Neurolaw in the Courtr

This collection presents a comparative perspective on interdisciplinary issues that fall under the emerging field of Neurolaw. The chapters embrace distinct procedural and evidential issues in the courtroom for vulnerable defendants, such as immature defendants, mentally disordered offenders and unfit-to-plead defendants, through a neuroscientific lens. This view is informed by worldwide analyses from legal academics, philosophers, and legal practitioners. The work brings together interdisciplinary and leading perspectives to discuss the use and relevancy of neuroscience at trial, and how the use of neuroscience is currently benefiting and impacting vulnerable defendants in global criminal trials. As such, the book builds upon and adds to the existing literature in this field by providing a comprehensive coverage of the intersection between these disciplines for vulnerable defendants in the courtroom. Key issues covered include: vulnerable defendants and the pre-trial process; the trial process; the use of neuroscience as expert evidence at trial; and vulnerable defendants, neuroscience and mitigation of sentence. Through original exploration presented by contributors from both academia and practice, the book will be of interest to academics, researchers and policy-makers working in the areas of Criminal Law and Procedure.

Hannah Wishart is a Lecturer in Law at the University of Sunderland and a PhD Candidate at the School of Law, University of Manchester.

Colleen M. Berryessa is an Assistant Professor at the Rutgers University School of Criminal Justice.

Routledge Contemporary Issues in Criminal Justice and Procedure

Series Editor **Ed Johnston** is an Associate Professor of Criminal Justice and Procedure at the University of Northampton, UK.

Vulnerability, the Accused, and the Criminal Justice System
Multijurisdictional Perspectives
Edited by Roxanna Dehaghani, Samantha Fairclough and Lore Mergaerts

Covid-19 and Criminal Justice
Impact and Legacy in England and Wales
Edited by Ed Johnston

Witness Protection and Criminal Justice in Africa
Nigeria in International Perspective
Suzzie Onyeka Oyakhire

Autism and Criminal Justice
The Experience of Suspects, Defendants and Offenders in England and Wales
Edited by Tom Smith

Robotics, AI and Criminal Law
Crimes against Robots
Kamil Mamak

Social Rehabilitation and Criminal Justice
Edited by Federica Coppola and Adriano Martufi

Neurolaw in the Courtroom
Comparative Perspectives on Vulnerable Defendants
Edited by Hannah Wishart and Colleen M. Berryessa

See more at https://www.routledge.com/Routledge-Research-in-Legal-History/book-series/CONTEMPCJP

Neurolaw in the Courtroom

Comparative Perspectives on
Vulnerable Defendants

**Edited by Hannah Wishart and
Colleen M. Berryessa**

Routledge
Taylor & Francis Group

LONDON AND NEW YORK

First published 2024
by Routledge
4 Park Square, Milton Park, Abingdon, Oxon OX14 4RN

and by Routledge
605 Third Avenue, New York, NY 10158

Routledge is an imprint of the Taylor & Francis Group, an informa business

British Library Cataloguing-in-Publication Data
A catalogue record for this book is available from the British Library

ISBN: 978-1-032-36267-0 (hbk)
ISBN: 978-1-032-36270-0 (pbk)
ISBN: 978-1-003-33105-6 (ebk)

DOI: 10.4324/9781003331056

Typeset in Galliard
by Deanta Global Publishing Services, Chennai, India

Contents

3   Vulnerable Defendants: Redefining Decision-Making through the Lenses of Neuroscience, Law and Artificial Intelligence   37

AMEDEO SANTOSUOSSO AND MATILDE GIUSTINIANI

4   Safeguarding the Procedural Rights of Young Defendants in England and Wales: The Role of Neuroscience   51

AMY SIXSMITH

5   Criminal Insanity in Norwegian Law between Care and Societal Protection   70

SOFIA MORATTI

Contributors

Colleen M. Berryessa is an Assistant Professor at the Rutgers University School of Criminal Justice. She utilises both qualitative and quantitative methods to consider how psychological processes, perceptions, attitudes, and social contexts affect the criminal justice system, particularly related to courts, sentencing, and forms of punishment broadly defined. She received a Ph.D. in Criminology from the University of Pennsylvania, a B.A. in Government and Mind, Brain, and Behavior from Harvard University, and served as a CIRGE research fellow at Stanford University.

Federica Coppola is an Assistant Professor of Law at IE Law School in Madrid and a Research Affiliate at the Department of Criminal Law at the Max Planck Institute for the Study of Crime, Security, and Law. Her research and teaching interests include criminal law theory, sentencing and punishment, criminal constitutional law, criminal and social justice, and neurolaw. She is the author of "*The Emotional Brain and the Guilty Mind: Novel Paradigms of Culpability and Punishment*" (Hart Publishing, 2021) and the co-editor of "Social Rehabilitation and Criminal Justice" (Routledge, in press). Her second monograph, "The Real Pain of Punishment: Eradicating Social Exclusion from Criminal Justice", is under contract with Cambridge University Press. Federica earned a J.D. from the University of Bologna Law School in 2010, an LL.M. in Comparative, European, and International Laws from the European University Institute in 2014, and a Ph.D. in law from the European University Institute in 2017.

Deborah W. Denno is the Arthur A. McGivney Professor of Law and Founding Director of the Neuroscience and Law Center at Fordham Law School. She received her B.A. from the University of Virginia, M.A. from the University of Toronto, and Ph.D. and J.D. from the University of Pennsylvania. Before joining the Fordham Law faculty, Professor Denno clerked for Anthony J. Scirica, formerly Chief Judge of the Third Circuit Court of Appeals, and worked as an associate at Simpson, Thacher & Bartlett. At Fordham Law School, she primarily teaches criminal law, criminal procedure, and various seminars on advanced criminal law topics, including a criminal law speaker series. Seven of Professor Denno's articles have been cited by the United States Supreme Court, some multiple times. Professor Denno contends that, when used correctly, neuroscience can contribute to more comprehensive and accurate assessments of a defendant's blameworthiness and, therefore, greater fairness in the criminal justice system.

Matilde Giustiniani, B.A. in Psychology, New York University, NY, USA; M.A. in Psychology, Neuroscience and Human Sciences, Department of Brain and Behavioral Sciences of the University of Pavia (DBBS) and Department of Humanities and Life Sciences of the University School for Advanced Studies (IUSS) Pavia.

Sjors Ligthart is Assisstant Professor of Criminal Law at Tilburg University and postdoc at Utrecht University, The Netherlands.

Gerben Meynen is the Chair of Forensic Psychiatry, Willem Pompe Institute for Criminal Law and Criminology, Utrecht University & Chair Ethics, in particular bioethics, Department of Philosophy, Faculty of Humanities, VU University Amsterdam, The Netherlands.

Sofia Moratti is an Associate Professor at the Department of Interdisciplinary Studies of Culture, Norwegian University of Science and Technology, Trondheim, Norway. Her research interests include the study of value-laden decision-making processes in professional settings; the Ethical, Legal and Social Implications (ELSI) of new technology; the evolution of professional authority, autonomy and self-regulation under technological or societal change. Moratti has a Ph.D. from the Department of Legal Theory, Sociology and Philosophy of Law, University of Groningen (the Netherlands). She was a "Max Weber" Fellow and later a Senior Researcher (Research Associate) at the European University Institute, where she conducted multiple projects on neuroscience in criminal justice, particularly on the insanity defence. Her professional experiences include membership of national and international Research Ethics Boards.

Amedeo Santosuosso is one of the founders and current Scientific Director of the European Center for Law, Science and New Technologies (ECLT) at the University of Pavia (I). He is Extraordinary Professor of Law, Science and New Technologies at the Department of Law, University of Pavia, and at the Institute for Advanced Study of Pavia (IUSS). He also served as President of the First Chamber at the Court of Appeal of Milan. Santosuosso has served in several ad hoc committees appointed by the Italian government on science and law issues. He was President of the European Association for Neuroscience and

Law (EANL) from its foundation (2010) till 2016 and is the main organizer of the Law, Neuroscience and New Technologies Winter School, which takes place yearly at the University of Pavia.

Amy Sixsmith is a senior lecturer in law and has taught law at the University of Sunderland for over 12 years. She is also a Senior Fellow of the Higher Education Academy (Advance HE). She has taught a wide range of subjects, including the English legal system, child law, family law, and medical law. She is heavily involved in coaching students as part of Sunderland Law School's wide range of extracurricular activities. She is involved in mooting, student negotiation, and client Interviewing. She has also acted as a judge for the National Client Interviewing Competition and the International Client Consultation Competition. Her primary research interest is children's rights, and she is currently undertaking a Ph.D. which focuses on children's rights in the context of the youth justice system.

Hannah Wishart is a Lecturer in Law at the University of Sunderland and a Ph.D. Candidate at the School of Law, University of Manchester. Her Ph.D. focuses on developmentally immature children, neuroscience, and diminished responsibility defence. She is the co-editor of this book. She has published peer-review journal articles on the relevancy of neuroscience in youth justice, the abolition of the doctrine of *doli incapax* and the unfair treatment of developmentally immature children in the English criminal justice system. Her research interests include youth justice, neurolaw, legal defences and adolescent brain development. She has previously worked at the University of Sunderland and the University of Manchester.

Table of Statutes

Table of Cases

Abbreviations

AI:	Artificial Intelligence
C.T:	Computerised Tomography
Crim:	PD Criminal Practice Directions
Crim:	PR Criminal Procedure Rules
ECHR:	European Convention on Human Rights
ECtHR:	European Court on Human Rights
EEG:	Electroencephalogram
FASD:	Fetal Alcohol Spectrum Disorders
ML:	Machine Learning
MRI:	Magnetic Resonance Imaging
PET:	Positron Emission Tomography
TBI:	Traumatic Brain Injury
tDCS:	Transcranial Direct Current Stimulation
U.S:	United States of America
WHO:	World Health Organization

Introduction

This edited collection offers a global perspective on interdisciplinary issues that fall under the new and emerging field of neurolaw. The chapters embrace distinct procedural and evidential issues in the courtroom for vulnerable defendants through a neuroscientific lens to discuss the relevance of neuroscience at trial and how neuroscience is currently benefiting and impacting vulnerable defendants in global criminal trials.

The field of *neurolaw* explores and synthesises relationships between the law and neuroscience and how these relationships may bear on legal contexts. Research pairing neuroscience – the study of the structure and function of the brain, neural systems, and related biological processes – with the law does not intend to illuminate or solve all the problems and issues that the law and its applications pose. Instead, neuroscientific advances can help us better understand human cognition, behaviour and, correspondingly, how such phenomena can and potentially *should* be handled in legal systems. This arguably may lead to better functioning and fairer justice systems worldwide.

More equitable and just outcomes in legal processes may be especially relevant to, and important for, *vulnerable defendants* – offenders who may require special legal protections, support, considerations, or care in criminal trials because of their age, mental status, or other personal characteristics – whose qualities are commonly misunderstood or not fully contemplated within their legal processes and outcomes. Indeed, neuroscience cannot answer all of the law's problems. Yet, as the contributions in this collection demonstrate, unique and novel arguments have arisen about mental (in)competency, guilt, and legal insanity with applying neuroscientific evidence to the international courtroom in criminal law. Thus, neuroscience has the potential to meaningfully inform procedural and evidential issues for vulnerable defendants in criminal trials within various international jurisdictions.

These chapters provide worldwide analyses of issues related to vulnerable defendants from legal academics, philosophers, and legal practitioners based in the United States (U.S.), the Netherlands, Italy, England, Norway, and Germany. In Chapter 1, Deborah W. Denno examines how different international legal systems treat vulnerable defendants through a comparative and systematic analysis of empirical work on neuroscientific

DOI: 10.4324/9781003331056-1

evidence in criminal cases in Canada, England and Wales, the Netherlands, Slovenia, and the United States. This includes discussing the different neurotechniques and issues these legal systems often face. In Chapter 2, Sjors Ligthart and Gerben Meynen engage with legal and ethical concepts, including coercion and a defendant's fundamental legal rights, to consider whether vulnerable defendants should be offered neurotechnologies in legal contexts and whether they would ever be able to provide valid consent when accepting such offers in exchange for lighter criminal sentences. In Chapter 3, Amedeo Santosuosso and Matilde Giustiniani discuss factors that may influence decision-making processes in cases involving vulnerable defendants and how the potential introduction of new technologies into the legal system, especially artificial intelligence (AI), may function or play important future roles within the legal system and its frameworks moving forward for these defendants. In Chapter 4, Amy Sixsmith argues that the legal mechanisms in England and Wales used to address the barriers to effective legal participation by vulnerable defendants, specifically defendants under 18 years of age, are inadequate. She highlights how neuroscientific research could and should be used to develop more effective and robust legal safeguards for defendants under 18 years of age. In Chapter 5, Sofia Moratti takes a socio-legal perspective to detail the process, debates, and legal considerations surrounding recent reforms made to the Norwegian legal system's determination and management of vulnerable defendants found or argued to be criminally insane. She describes how these developments raise ethical and legal questions about the divergence and relationships between law and medicine and that these issues are unlikely to be addressed by neuroscience in the future. Finally, in Chapter 6, Federica Coppola explores the relevance and necessity of bringing neuroscientific understandings of trauma into sentencing processes in cases involving vulnerable defendants with chronic or repeated exposure to severe social adversity. She argues that sentencing systems must be sensitive to the traumatising effects of social vulnerability to address defendants' individual needs and to promote fairness and equality in their punishments.

Ultimately – ranging from pre-trial and trial processes to the insanity defence to the use of neuroscience in expert evidence during sentencing – the topics and coverage provided within these contributions offer a comprehensive, meaningful, and unmatched collection of work on vulnerable defendants in the criminal courtroom that sits at the intersection of law, philosophy, and neuroscience. We certainly hope that the readers of these chapters will gain significant insight into neuroscience's current and future roles in the courtroom involving vulnerable defendants worldwide and how its use may impact their legal and other life outcomes. Indeed, this collection is a first step in considering how neuroscience may better the legal trajectories of defendants from some of society's most vulnerable groups across the globe.

1 Vulnerable Defendants and Neuroscience in Courtrooms Worldwide

Deborah W. Denno

1.1 Introduction

The increasing prevalence of neuroscience in courtrooms worldwide is especially striking in criminal cases involving mentally vulnerable defendants.[1] Defendants classified as mentally vulnerable can manifest a broad scope of cognitive and learning disorders that hinder efforts to follow social and legal rules and prompt entanglement with the criminal system.[2] Yet, defence attorneys confront daunting challenges in their attempts to prove the nature and extent of these disorders. As such, neuroscientific evidence, most broadly understood "as any information related to the brain," becomes a crucial legal tool, particularly when vulnerable defendants are involved.[3]

Given the significance of this neuroscience–vulnerability link – and the dearth of research available on it – this chapter examines how different criminal justice systems treat vulnerable defendants through a comparative analysis of empirical research on neuroscientific evidence in criminal cases. The discussion focuses on five systematic studies: one carried out in

---

1 T. Spranger (ed), *International Neurolaw: A Comparative Analysis* (Springer-Verlag Berlin Heidelberg, 2012 edn); D. W. Denno, 'Empirical Use of Neuroscientific Evidence in Criminal Justice' in *The Encyclopedia of Behavioral Neuroscience* (2nd ed) (Elsevier, Amsterdam, Netherlands: Sergio Della Salla, 2022 ed) 719.

2 H. Howard, 'Effective Participation of Mentally Vulnerable Defendants in the Magistrate Courts in England and Wales – The Front Line from a Legal Perspective' (2021) 85 (1) *The Journal of Criminal Law* 3. <https://journals.sagepub.com/doi/full/10.1177/0022018320957110>.

3 D. Aono, G. Yaffe, and H. Kober, 'Neuroscientific Evidence in the Courtroom: A Review' (2019) 4(40) *Cognitive Res.: Principles and Implications* 3. Other references have more specific definitions of "neuroscience." According to one source, for example, "neuroscience" is "[t]he scientific study of the structure and function of the nervous system; includes experimental and clinical studies of animals and humans." O. D. Jones, J. D. Schall and F. X. Shen, Law and Neuroscience (2nd Edn, Aspen Publishing 2020) 931.

DOI: 10.4324/9781003331056-2

the U.S.[4] and the others conducted in five additional countries – Canada,[5] England and Wales,[6] the Netherlands[7] and Slovenia.[8]

This international approach gives a new lens to defendant vulnerability by deciphering the techniques and hurdles different criminal justice systems face and the solutions they seek. It also provides a vehicle for framing the picture of "vulnerability" in light of the term's definitional vagueness. Whether neuroscience can come to the rescue remains to be seen, yet such a proposition makes sense morally, legally and pragmatically.

Section 1.2 examines the meaning and definitions of a vulnerable defendant, especially those who are mentally vulnerable. Section 1.3 compares the five international studies probing the use of neuroscientific evidence in cases of mentally vulnerable defendants to establish the breadth of this global framework and perspective. Section 1.4 illustrates the link between vulnerability and neuroscience and how legal systems have responded to mentally vulnerable defendants, focusing on one English case. Section 1.5 recommends ways neuroscience can contribute to the legal system's treatment of vulnerable defendants.

1.2 What Is a "Vulnerable Defendant"?

English sources delineate the terms "vulnerable defendants" or "vulnerable people" in more detail than sources in the U.S. or other countries.[9]

---

4 D. W. Denno, 'The Myth of the Double-Edged Sword: An Empirical Study of Neuroscience Evidence in Criminal Cases' (2015) 56(2) *Boston College Law Review* 493; D. W. Denno, 'How Experts Have Dominated the Neuroscience Narrative in Criminal Cases for Twelve Decades: A Warning for the Future' (2022) 63 *William & Mary Law Review* 1215.

5 J. A. Chandler, 'The Use of Neuroscientific Evidence in Canadian Criminal Proceedings' (2015) 2(3) *Journal of Law and the Biosciences* 550.

6 P. Catley, L. Claydon, 'The Use of Neuroscientific Evidence in the Courtroom by Those Accused of Criminal Offenses in England and Wales' (2015) 2(3) *Journal of Law and the Biosciences* 510.

7 C. H. de Kogel, E. J. M. C. Westgeest, 'Neuroscientific and behavioral genetic information in criminal cases in the Netherlands' (2015) 2(3) *Journal of Law and the Biosciences* 580.

8 M. Hafner, 'Judging Homicide Defendants by Their Brains: An Empirical Study on the Use of Neuroscience in Homicide Trials in Slovenia' (2019) 6(1) *Journal of Law and the Biosciences* 226.

9 The checking of a wide range of resources to seek a definition of "vulnerable defendants" in U.S. law comes up empty. Those checked resources included the following: Black's Law Dictionary, Ballentine's Law Dictionary, American Law Reports, CLE Materials, law review articles, and searches on Westlaw through legal encyclopedias. None of these materials provided a specific entry on "vulnerable defendants," although two resources used the term as a focus point. See T. R. Birkhead, K. R. Guest Pryal, 'Symposium 2014: Vulnerable Defendants in the Criminal Justice System' (2015) 93 *North Carolina Law Review* 1211; D. Collins, 'Reevaluating Competence to Stand Trial' (2019) 82 *Law and Contemporary Problems* 157.

The main focus among English references is individuals' mental – rather than physical – vulnerabilities. For example, according to the Consolidated Criminal Practice Direction of 2013 – part of a set of rules of procedure for criminal courts in England and Wales – the phrase "vulnerable people in the courts" is specified as follows: juveniles under age 18 "and people with a mental disorder or learning disability; a physical disorder or disability; or who are likely to suffer fear and distress in giving evidence because of their own circumstances or those relating to the case."[10]

Vulnerability is also a key topic in large-scale research. A recent qualitative study of lawyers representing clients in the magistrates' courts of England and Wales centred on the treatment of the "mentally vulnerable defendant," which the study "defined in the broadest sense to include the defendant suffering from any mental disorder/learning difficulty which might compromise his/her ability to stand trial."[11] Likewise, one of the most extensive studies analysing vulnerabilities among (over 9,000) defendants presented to the Court Mental Health Liaison and Diversion services particularly emphasised individuals "who present with major mental illness." In addition, that category could include other "vulnerable groups" such as those with neurodevelopmental disorders and substance and alcohol abuse."[12]

England and Wales have prioritised examining vulnerable individuals in the criminal justice system.[13] For instance, in 2022, His Majesty's Courts and Tribunals Service, responsible for administering civil, criminal, and family courts in England and Wales, put forth a Vulnerability Action Plan, which the government continuously updates.[14] Defining "vulnerable" people as those who could have a disability, "mental health condition," or "an experience" that could make them "feel unsafe," the action plan fosters courts and tribunals that are "accessible for everyone" and prevent discrimination.[15] However, even with a definition, the scope of the term "vulnerable people" is broad and encompassing.

---

10 *Criminal Practice Directions* [2013] EWCA Crim 1631 [8, Sec. 3D.1, 3D2], <https://www.judiciary.uk/wp-content/uploads/JCO/Documents/Practice+Directions/Consolidated-criminal/criminal-practice-directions-2013.pdf>.

11 Howard (n 2).

12 E. Chaplin et al., 'Severe Mental Illness, Common Mental Disorders, and Neurodevelopmental Conditions Amongst 9088 lower Court Attendees in London, UK' (2022) 22(551) *BMC Psychiatry* 2. <https://link.springer.com/content/pdf/10.1186/s12888-022-04150-4.pdf>.

13 R. K. Helm, 'Guilty Pleas in Children: Legitimacy, Vulnerability, and the Need for Increased Protection' (2021) 48(2) *Journal of Law and Society* 179.

14 HM Courts & Tribunal Services, 'HMCTS Vulnerability Action Plan' Policy Paper (Nov. 2022) <https://www.gov.uk/government/publications/hmcts-vulnerability-action-plan/hmcts-vulnerability-action-plan-october-2022-update>.

15 Ibid.

All countries have vulnerable defendants in their criminal justice systems that meet the criteria established in English laws and research. The punitive bent of the U.S. criminal justice, especially the U.S.'s embrace of harsh sentences and the death penalty, nets vulnerable defendants who face higher stakes than those in other Western countries.[16] For example, in 2022, U.S. executions disproportionately involved vulnerable individuals with significant mental health challenges, a finding consistent with past executions.[17] Thirteen of the 18 people executed in the U.S. in 2022 evidenced substantial mental illness, brain damage, intellectual disability, and chronic childhood trauma.[18] The absence of a comparatively broad term designating certain categories of defendants as "vulnerable" seemingly enables the U.S. system to punish such susceptible defendants harshly without adequate consideration and accountability for their physical and mental conditions.

Countries vary in their approaches to vulnerable defendants and their reliance on neuroscience in the context of changing punitive philosophies. This comparative lens is especially beneficial given the broad categories that English sources in particular proffer in their attempts to frame the meaning of mental vulnerability. Examining how different legal systems treat and consider neuroscientific evidence can sharpen that perspective.

1.3 International Research on Neuroscience and Defendant Vulnerability

Neuroscientific evidence is at the forefront of most legal cases involving potentially vulnerable individuals. This part explores five systematic and empirical studies of mentally vulnerable defendants to illustrate the significance of neuroscientific evidence in courtrooms across six countries: the U.S.,[19] Canada,[20] England and Wales,[21] the Netherlands[22] and Slovenia.[23] The studies had substantial methodological similarities, enhancing the opportunity to juxtapose them.

---

16 Birckhead (n 9); A. Corda, R. Hester, 'Leaving the Shining City on a Hill: A Plea for Rediscovering Comparative Criminal Justice Policy in the United States' (2021) 31(2) *International Criminal Justice Review* 203.
17 Death Penalty Information Center, 'The Death Penalty in 2022: Year End Report' (Dec. 16, 2022) 22 <https://deathpenaltyinfo.org/facts-and-research/dpic-reports/dpic-year-end-reports/the-death-penalty-in-2022-year-end-report>.
18 Ibid.
19 Denno (n 4).
20 Chandler (n 5).
21 Catley (n 6).
22 de Kogel (n 7).
23 Hafner (n 8).

As Table 1.1 shows, all studies empirically examined a country's use of neuroscientific evidence in criminal cases over time (ranging from 4 to 120 years) to demonstrate how and why courts use this information. While the number of criminal cases varied (from 89 to over 8,000), all the studies acquired their data by relying upon widely used legal databases, such as Westlaw and Lexis.[24] Hafner's Slovenia study ultimately culled out only homicide cases he obtained directly from the courts because his initial legal database search showed that attorneys introduced neuroscientific evidence in homicides more than other types of crimes.[25]

The other studies echoed Hafner's focus on homicides but also found a significant use of neuroscience with additional crimes of violence. In all countries, neuroscientific evidence was employed most frequently in homicides, various crimes of violence, and sexual offences; only a small percentage of cases involved drugs, property, or driving offences (Table 1.1). In the U.S., nearly one-half of defendants faced the death penalty, and the remainder were incarcerated for life or long sentences.[26]

Not surprisingly, studies defined "neuroscience" somewhat differently (Table 1.1). While neuroscience focuses on the brain and nervous system, there is no "universal definition" of what that research constitutes, given the broad range of disciplines involved.[27] Instead, researchers create a definition using search terms consistent with the information they collect and analyse in the context of the criminal cases they find in their legal databases.[28]

Nonetheless, most studies looked at two types of neuroscientific evidence:[29] (1) neuroimaging tests – which consist of "various techniques" including M.R.I., P.E.T. and E.E.G. "to directly or indirectly image the structure, function, and pharmacology of the brain"[30] – and (2) non-neuroimaging tests, such as psychometric tests, which assess brain structure and function without the use of imaging.[31] In all studies, most criminal cases also relied heavily on expert witnesses who testified with or without using tests, often discussing a defendant's medical and cognitive history, such as brain injuries and accidents (see Table 1.2).[32]

---

24 Denno (n 1) 720-21, Table 4.
25 Hafner (n 8) 229.
26 Denno (n 1).
27 Ibid 720.
28 Ibid 720-21.
29 Ibid 721.
30 Jones (n 3) 931.
31 Denno (n 1) 721.
32 Ibid.

Table 1.1 Study Methodology

Study	Country	Time-Span	Number of Cases	Definition of "Neuroscience"	Type Of Crime
Catley & Claydon (2015)	England & Wales	2005-2012 (8 years)	204	Cited the Royal Society's definition and focused on cases with a basis in cognitive neuroscience	Homicide; Crimes of violence; Crimes of dishonesty; Sexual offences; Drug offences; Driving offences; Other
Chandler (2015)	Canada	2008-2012 (5 years)	133	Excluded a definition but focused on cases involving evidence of brain injury or cognitive impairment linked to a neurological cause	Homicide; Crimes of violence; Sexual offences; Drug offences; Driving offences; Property offences; Other
Denno (2015)–(2020)	U.S.	1992-2012 (20 years) 1900-2020 (120 years)	800 8,358	Defined broadly as involving the brain and nervous system and provided an operationalized definition including imaging tests, non-imaging tests, and expert testimony	Death Penalty; Homicide; Crimes of violence; Sexual offences; Drug offences; Driving offences; Property offences; Crimes involving children; Other
Hafner (2019)	Slovenia	1991-2015 (24 years)	89	Examined cases discussing brain damage, neurological diseases and dysfunctions, or organic mental, personality, and behavioural disorders	Homicide only
de Kogel & Westgeest (2015)	The Netherlands	2000-2012 (12 years)	231	Defined as involving assessments of the brain, neuropsychological assessments, or neurobiological predisposition or brain damage; also included a separate definition for behavioural genetic information	Crimes of violence; Sexual offences; Drug offences; Property offences; Other

Table 1.2 Types of Neuroscientific Evidence Introduced

Study	Types of Evidence Introduced	Reliance on Neuroimaging
England & Wales Catley & Claydon (2015)	Neuroimaging; Head injury & brain damage; Family history; Cognitive impairment; Developmental immaturity; Alcohol dependency syndrome	Reported cases involving neuroimaging almost always used structural scans over functional scans. Types of scans included: E.E.G.; fM.R.I.; M.R.I.; C.A.T./C.T. scan; P.E.T. scan; S.P.E.C.T. scan; Brain scan
Canada Chandler (2015)	Prenatal alcohol exposure; Neuropsychological testing; Traumatic brain injuries; Neuroimaging; Dementia; Epilepsy; Birth trauma; Parasomnia; Tumor	Included neuroimaging in the search terms but such imaging was infrequently mentioned in the cases
U.S. Denno (2015)— (2020)	Brain damage; Head injury; Low IQ/mental retardation; Toxic exposure; Neuroimaging; Adult personality/ behavioural disorders; Mental/ behavioural disorders due to psychoactive substance abuse; Organic mental disorders; Schizophrenia, schizotypal, and delusional disorders	Discussed neuroimaging tests in nearly two-thirds of the defendant cases with death penalty cases being the most common
Slovenia Hafner (2019)	Brain damage; Age-related impairments; Neurological diseases and dysfunctions; Organic mental disorders; Organic personality disorders; Behavioural disorders; Neuroimaging	Noted that only four cases mentioned structural brain imaging and five cases mentioned E.E.G. tests. There was no recorded functional neuroimaging among the reviewed cases
The Netherlands de Kogel & Westgeest (2015)	Neuroimaging; Neuro-endocrinological assessment; Neurobiological predisposition; Damage to the brain; Heritability factors; Genetic predisposition; Family history indicating biological origin; Addiction	Detailed that 42% of cases involved some form of neuroimaging

Table 1.3 Purpose and Use of Neuroscientific Evidence in Criminal Proceedings

Study	Court Opinion from which Cases were Pulled	Phase of Criminal Proceeding where Neuroscience was Used	Stage of Court Proceeding where Neuroscience was Most Used	Most Common Purpose for Neuroscientific Evidence	Most Common Purpose for Mitigating Neuroscientific Evidence	Prosecutor's Use of Neuroscientific Evidence
England & Wales Catley & Claydon (2015)	Appellate	Pre-trial; Guilt; Sentencing	Sentencing	Aggravation by way of victim evidence	Used to quash convictions, to lead to convictions for lesser offences, and to lead to reduced sentences with the most successful application during appeals of sentence	Employed by the prosecution to provide evidence of a victim's injuries or cause of death or injury; however, the study's focus concerned the defence's use of mitigating evidence
Canada Chandler (2015)	First Instance; Appellate; Supreme	Pre-trial; Guilt; Sentencing	Sentencing	Mitigation	Employed for assessing moral blameworthiness during the sentencing phase, particularly for violent crimes	Excluded any discussion of the prosecution's use of neuroscientific evidence
U.S. Denno (2015)—(2020)	Appellate (and some trial)	Pre-trial; Guilt; Sentencing (penalty for death penalty cases)	Sentencing (mostly for death penalty cases)	Mitigation	Implemented to mitigate punishments, especially during the penalty phase for death penalty cases	Reported it was rare for prosecutors to use neuroscientific evidence to suggest a defendant's propensity to commit crimes, but when they did, they typically built on evidence that was introduced by the defence
Slovenia Hafner (2019)	District; Appellate; Supreme	Pre-trial; Guilt; Sentencing	Sentencing	Mitigation	Applied to mitigate or reduce sentencing	Excluded any discussion of the prosecution's use of neuroscientific evidence, but did report that neuroscientific evidence was never used as an aggravating factor
The Netherlands de Kogel & Westgeest (2015)	First Instance; Appellate; Supreme	Pre-trial; Guilt; Sentencing	Sentencing	Mitigation	Incorporated to show diminished accountability for the offence	Excluded any discussion of the prosecution's use of neuroscientific evidence

The phase at which attorneys present evidence is also significant. In all studies, attorneys introduce neuroscientific evidence in every phase of a criminal proceeding – pre-trial, guilt, and sentencing (see Table 1.3). However, depending on the country, neuroscientific evidence may be more widely used and influential at some phases than others, especially in the U.S., where sentencing is a critical component of death penalty cases.[33] For all but one study, the most common purpose for neuroscientific evidence was to mitigate the crime or the sentence (Table 1.3). The exception – Catley and Claydon's study of England and Wales[34] – explained that prosecutors could use neuroscientific evidence to aggravate a defendant's sentence by clarifying the extent of the victim's injuries or cause of death (see Table 1.3). Denno's U.S. study also found that prosecutors incorporate the evidence for a similar purpose (the victim's injuries) but with less frequency.[35] While other studies did not mention a prosecutor's employment of neuroscientific evidence or found it rare, these revelations demonstrate how such evidence may work against vulnerable defendants in some cases (see Table 1.3).

1.4 How Neuroscience Works in Vulnerable Defendant Cases

Neuroscientific evidence can contribute to the law in a range of ways.[36] This chapter's examination of five international studies illuminates how different legal systems use neuroscientific evidence in criminal cases involving vulnerable defendants and how courts frame it to support a decision typically reached on appeal. For example, in all study countries, a defendant's blameworthiness depends on their mental state, which their level of vulnerability can substantially influence.

Reviewing the elements of a crime, such as a homicide, can illustrate the legal dynamics of the neuroscience–vulnerability link. Generally, each crime has two key components: the *mens rea*, which refers to the defendant's mental state at the time of the offence, and the *actus reus*, which refers to the defendant's voluntary act that causes social harm. For example, if A intentionally picks up a gun and shoots B, A has performed a voluntary act (shooting B) that caused B's death (the social harm), and A did so intentionally (the mental state). While criminal law supposes that most human behaviour is voluntary and that individuals are consciously aware

---

33 Ibid 726–27; Hafner (n 8) 243-44.
34 Catley (n 6).
35 D. W. Denno, 'Concocting Criminal Intent' (2017) 105(2) *Georgetown Law Journal* 323.
36 O. D. Jones, et al., 'Law and Neuroscience' (2013) 33(45) *The Journal of Neuroscience* 17624.

of their acts, it also recognises that individuals who act unconsciously, such as those experiencing a reflex response, are simply not acting. Under the criminal law's voluntary act requirement, courts can acquit unconscious individuals even if their behaviour results in severe harm.[37]

There are different degrees of *mens rea* that, if proven, can potentially change the crime for which the defendant has been charged or mitigate a sentence based partly on neuroscientific evidence.[38] For example, Catley and Claydon's study of England and Wales (Tables 1.1–1.3) discusses *R v Hendy*, a diminished responsibility case in which a jury convicted the 16-year-old defendant of murder after he stabbed a stranger 18 times with a knife during an unprovoked attack.[39] On appeal, the defence's purpose in arguing the defence of diminished responsibility was to reduce Hendy's conviction of murder to manslaughter.[40]

While there is no general legal definition of "diminished responsibility" (or, in the U.S., "diminished capacity"), courts have accepted the defence based on two different rationales in assessing a defendant's guilt. First, courts acknowledge the defence's use "as a basis for admitting evidence concerning the defendant's mental disease, defect, condition or abnormality at the time of the offense to show that the defendant lacked or possessed the required mental state for the crime."[41] Second, courts regard diminished responsibility "as a basis for mitigating the seriousness of an offense, because of the defendant's mental disease, defect, condition or abnormality at the time of the crime, in order to render him or her guilty of a less serious offense."[42] Attorneys can also present such evidence as a mitigating factor in sentencing, including death penalty cases.[43]

In *Hendy*, the defence's neuroscientific evidence was varied. Testifying experts explained that Hendy experienced a head injury from a road accident that "may have caused damage to [his] temporal lobe, that part of his brain which governs temper control and learning."[44] To emphasise the complicated role of Hendy's heavy drinking on the night of the crime, experts specified that Hendy's "use of alcohol was a symptom of his emotional problems and not their cause."[45] Notably, after Hendy's

---

37 Denno (n 35).
38 D. W. Denno, 'Neuroscience and the Personalization of Criminal Law' (2019) 86(2) *The University of Chicago Law Review* 359.
39 Catley (n 6) 525–526 (discussing *R v Hendy* [2006] EWCA 819).
40 Ibid.
41 D. M. Siegel, 'The Defense of Diminished Capacity,' in R. Cipes, S. Bernstein, and E. Hall, 1B (eds) *Criminal Defense Techniques* § 32.01(1)(e) (Matthew Bender & Co 2018).
42 Ibid.
43 Ibid.
44 Catley (n 6) 526.
45 Ibid.

1993 conviction, he was administered an E.E.G. that indicated left temporal lobe damage, a finding bolstered by later neuropsychometric testing. This new evidence, along with the information on Hendy's head injury and a diagnosis of depression, convinced the Court of Appeal to overturn Hendy's murder conviction, substituting it with a manslaughter conviction by reason of the defence of diminished responsibility.[46] Hendy was not acquitted but was provided with a hospital order during sentencing under the Mental Health Act of 1983.[47]

According to Catley and Claydon, *Hendy* exemplifies how a court may use neuroscientific evidence by considering a broad spectrum of information and issues. These include known mental disorders, problems associated with developmental immaturity in light of Hendy's young age, and the impact of intoxicants.[48] The *Hendy* court's ultimate disposition is more troubling, however. While "evidence of neurocognitive defects" made it so that Hendy avoided a criminal conviction, it seemingly also prompted "an elevated view" of Hendy's risk of harm, which resulted in the court's "imposition of a restriction order without limit of time."[49] How long Hendy could be under a restricted hospital order is unclear, but the outcome may not necessarily be more favourable than a criminal conviction for manslaughter.

Hendy illustrates some significant factors that may arise when the legal system confronts neuroscientific evidence involving vulnerable defendants. The next part discusses what neuroscientific evidence can and cannot contribute to aiding the legal system's treatment of vulnerable defendants.

1.5 Ways Neuroscience Can Contribute to the Legal System's Treatment of Vulnerable Defendants

Countries vary in their use of neuroscientific evidence based on their "unique legal, historical, and sociocultural" makeups.[50] This part considers how neuroscience can contribute to a legal system's treatment of vulnerable defendants in at least three overlapping ways that can enhance alternatives to punishment and efficiency.

---

46 Ibid 527.
47 Ibid; see Mental Health Act of 1983, ss 37 and 41.
48 Catley (n 6) 527.
49 Ibid.
50 F. X. Shen, 'Neuroscientific Evidence as Instant Replay,' (2016) 3 *Journal of Law and the Biosciences* 343, 346.

1.5.1 *Clarifying the Definition of Defendant Vulnerability*

Defendant vulnerability is an amorphous concept, as this chapter notes. For defendants who are mentally vulnerable, the term can include juveniles under the age of 18 or individuals with a mental disorder, learning disability, major mental illness, or problem with substance or alcohol abuse. The vagueness of such conditions is understandable in legal sources and research studies that aim to create broadly inclusive categories. Yet, this approach can lack substance in a legal setting. As a result, judges and juries may not know how to identify vulnerable people and empathise with them, seeing them in a far more punitive light than they deserve.

Neuroscientific evidence can help clarify the meaning of a defendant's mental vulnerability. For example, as *R v Hendy* demonstrates, a substantial amount of research exists specifying the brain-behaviour underpinnings of recognised mental disorders, issues of developmental immaturity, and the relationship between intoxicants and responsibility for criminal acts.

Alternatively, for some, evidence of neurocognitive defects can also heighten the likelihood that judges and jurors may perceive a defendant as a danger to others. In these circumstances, the appellant's team can use neuroscientific evidence "to challenge previous explanations of the appellant's behavior or to question previous psychological or psychiatric assessments of the [appellant's] risk or dangerousness."[51]

Research in the Netherlands by de Kogel and Westgeest notes that in some cases, a defendant's head injury or brain damage indicates they were "extra vulnerable" to an extreme emotional state, prompting attorneys' use of a particular defence.[52] For example, in one assault case, defence attorneys contended that the defendant engaged in "excessive self-defence" because he suffered a concussion when the victim hit him in the head, thus creating the defendant's "strong emotional state" that led him to hit the victim back. While the appellate courts generally have not accepted defence arguments concerning increased vulnerability, such resistance was not necessarily because of the concept. Instead, it "appears that the claims that the defendant was extra vulnerable for a strong emotional state or (excessive) self-defence do not seem to be substantiated further by tests of mental capacities of the defendant or other evidence."[53] Thus, had attorneys introduced more relevant neuroscientific evidence,

---

51 Catley (n 6) 515.
52 de Kogel (n 7) 596.
53 Ibid 597.

the courts would have been more likely to accept arguments that defendants were extra vulnerable to heightened emotional states.

The Dutch courts' conclusions raise another issue. What kind of neuroscientific evidence would convince courts or juries that a defendant was vulnerable, much less "extra vulnerable"? Tables 1.1–1.3 indicate that the cases in all five studies broadly defined "neuroscience" to incorporate the incredible range of evidence that attorneys introduce in court. While neuroimaging was a component of the neuroscientific evidence in each study, it was rarely introduced alone. Instead, attorneys would present a range of evidence, including non-neuroimaging tests, expert testimony, medical records, proof of toxin exposure, etc. There is no singular definition of neuroscience or the methods to measure it.

One challenge is that courts and attorneys are not always well versed in neuroscientific evidence, to the detriment of the mentally vulnerable defendant. An example of this circumstance is shown in *R v Gwaza*, an English case decided a few years after *Hendy*. In *Gwaza*, a trial judge emphasised the *absence* of brain scans by the defence as a rationale for sentencing Gwaza to indefinite detention for the public's protection.[54] As the court explained, Gwaza "refused to be examined" and also "refused to have a brain scan, or any other test which might" indicate that he was "suffering from some real illness."[55] Therefore, the court was limited to concluding that Gwaza's psychotic disorder and attack on another person resulted from his taking cannabis. If Gwaza consumed cannabis again, there was "every likelihood" he would "suffer a similar psychotic disorder," even if he were released after a five-year term of imprisonment, which the court would give him "in the normal course of events."[56]

On appeal, Gwaza followed the trial judge's wishes. He acquired a C.T. scan, indicating that his "brain appear[ed] physically normal . . . and there was no evidence that there was an organic cause for the acute mental illness he suffered at the time of his arrest."[57] As a result, the appellate court *reduced* Gwaza's sentence and removed the condition of indefinite detention. This outcome was in direct contrast to the trial judge who referred to the absence of a brain scan as part of the reason for sentencing Gwaza to indefinite detention for public protection.

Gwaza illustrates how intricate and multi-faceted neuroscientific evidence can be in a case involving numerous factors. Ultimately, however, the appellate court was persuaded by other evidence indicating

---

54 Catley (n 6) 535. Indefinite detention is typically call "IPP," or imprisonment for public protection (IPP).
55 Ibid 535 (discussing *R v Gwaza* [2009] EWCA Crim 1101).
56 Ibid.
57 Ibid.

that Gwaza would not be a substantial risk of harm to the public. As the study's authors explain, this twist "highlights the fact that neuroscientific evidence is only one part of the argument presented to the court; other evidence may be more convincing."[58] Such a conclusion could also clarify the definition of vulnerable defendants.

1.5.2 Examining the Impact of the "Double-Edged Sword"

Much of the debate concerning the intersection of neuroscience and criminal law centres on the belief that courts will treat neuroscientific evidence as a potential "double-edged sword." For example, some commentators assume neuroscientific evidence will help abdicate violent criminals of all responsibility for their crimes. In contrast, others fear such evidence could buttress predictions of defendants' purported future danger to society, thus unfairly increasing their levels of punishment. Chandler explains the dynamic further. "Neuroscientific evidence suggesting diminished capacity tends to reduce moral blameworthiness . . . and yet it also tends to increase judgements about risk and dangerousness, given the view . . . that brain injuries can sometimes be managed but not cured."[59] In short, "a brain *too* broken may be simply too dangerous to have at large, even *if* it is somehow less culpable."[60] *Hendy* illustrates this scenario well. There, the court was concerned about the defendant's diminished capacity *and* risk of dangerousness based on neuroscientific evidence of the defendant's vulnerability.

Most studies this chapter discusses did not fully support the concept of a double-edged sword or report that prosecutors used neuroscience as an aggravating factor. According to Hafner's study of Slovenia, neuroscience was never introduced as an aggravating factor among Slovenian homicide cases, and there was "no evidence of the double-edged sword of neuroscience effect."[61] While defendants were sentenced to compulsory psychiatric treatment in about one-fifth of the cases involving neuroscientific evidence, the purpose of such a judgement was not meant to be punitive.[62] Instead, the criminal justice system aimed to protect society and rehabilitate the defendant.[63] Likewise, even though neuroscientific evidence was introduced to prove a defendant's potential

---

58 Ibid 536 (discussing Gwaza [2009]).
59 Chandler (n 5) 574.
60 O. D. Jones, F. X. Shen, 'Law and Neuroscience in the United States,' in Spranger (2012 ed.) 349, p. 362.
61 Hafner (n 8) 239-40.
62 Ibid 241.
63 Ibid.

dangerousness in about one-quarter of the cases, this approach was never intended to justify a longer or harsher sentence "in the same way as observers of the double-edged sword effect report for other countries."[64]

Denno's U.S. studies also did not provide systematic evidence of a double-edged sword framework. Only rarely was a defendant's potential for future dangerousness an aspect of cases involving neuroscientific evidence.[65] Instead, defence attorneys most commonly presented neuroscientific evidence to mitigate a defendant's sentence and support a claim of ineffective assistance of counsel based on a trial attorney omitting or misusing such evidence.[66]

The other studies reported more equivocal results. For example, while Catley and Claydon's study of England and Wales did not explicitly address the "double-edged sword" concept, it did report that the prosecution (not the defence) was more likely to introduce neuroscientific evidence to examine the victim's brain damage.[67] Neuroscientific evidence could better detail the victim's injuries or cause of death, reinforcing the prosecution's recommendations for the defendant's sentence.[68]

Chandler's Canadian study reported divergent outcomes. Neuroscientific evidence either hindered (34%) or mitigated (38%) sentencing decisions in criminal cases to nearly the same extent.[69] Likewise, some courts cited neuroscientific evidence to justify enhancing a defendant's sentence;[70] yet, in other cases, courts viewed the evidence as mitigating.[71]

Lastly, while de Kogel and Westgeest's Netherlands study confirmed the existence of a double-edged sword framework, they emphasised that this effect may be strongest "in cases with a high risk of severe violence."[72] That said, courts were still open to evidence demonstrating defendants' opportunities to reduce their risk of recidivating.

Most studies did not find the double-edged sword concept to be as solid and consistent as many commentators first surmised. Yet, the concept remains a stable framework for some courts.

What does this situation say about the criminal justice system's treatment of vulnerable defendants? Chandler's study of Canada may provide

---

64 Ibid 241-42.
65 Denno (n 4) 494.
66 Ibid 499, 525.
67 Catley (n 6) 515.
68 Ibid; Denno's study also made such a finding about victims but not in the context of a double-edged sword argument. Denno (n 35).
69 Chandler (n 5) 569.
70 Ibid 574.
71 Ibid 569-70.
72 de Kogel (n 7) 601.

some clues. Her research included examining a specific type of mentally vulnerable defendant – those affected by fetal alcohol spectrum disorders (FASDs).[73] As Chandler explains, "evidence related to brain damage flowing from prenatal alcohol exposure is the most common form of evidence considered [in the Canadian criminal justice system], followed by medical history of TBI [traumatic brain injury] and neuropsychological testing."[74] While this evidence mostly mitigates, Chandler highlighted its double-edged sword nature, prompting some courts to view affected defendants as a future risk.

What contributes to this double-edged perspective for vulnerable defendants in Canada? One answer is the lack of existing alternatives to incarceration. Chandler's research shows that, even when Canadian judges accept that a defendant's brain damage mitigates their legal blameworthiness, there may not be suitable services for treatment and containment, especially for brain-damaged defendants who may be a high risk. This circumstance thwarts efforts towards criminal justice reforms that Chandler believes should apply to all mentally vulnerable defendants, not just those who are FASD-affected.[75]

1.5.3 Considering Legal Reforms for Vulnerable Defendants

There is a need for tailored treatment and rehabilitation options for vulnerable defendants. Neuroscientific evidence can help in this process but cannot answer all questions, nor should it. For example, several studies noted that courts requested more neuroscientific evidence and explanation in cases than experts could readily provide. Hafner reports "it was evident in a number of cases that courts sought and expected more information from neuroscience experts on the question of how a particular brain dysfunction affected the defendant's concrete mental and cognitive capacities."[76] Yet, these experts "were seldom able to provide such a definitive answer that could be simply subsumed under one of the [mental health] categories."[77]

Consequently, courts turn to incarceration or, as in *Hendy*, a hospital order in which a defendant's time limits and restrictions are unclear. The Slovenian criminal justice system, which shuns a double-edged sword perspective, offers some potential guidance. It provides two medical security measures that give defendants as much liberty as possible and strive to keep them out of prison. Further, courts must assess defendants every

---

73 Chandler (n 5).
74 Ibid 557.
75 Ibid 574.
76 Hafner (n 8) 244.
77 Ibid.

six months to determine if a medical security measure is still needed. Lastly, the legal system must cease compulsory psychiatric treatment and confinement in a mental health institution after five years so that such a placement "can no longer be extended as a criminal sanction."[78] In this context, neuroscientific information can help determine the extent to which an offender may be a risk or which treatment program may be more beneficial.

The Slovenian criminal justice system also rests on a different foundational premise. Hafner emphasises that criminal justice actors do not use neuroscientific evidence to remove or isolate defendants – quite the contrary. He has observed that "the attitude of the Slovenian criminal justice system towards perpetrators of homicides with brain dysfunctions could perhaps be characterized as optimistic, idealistic, or paternalistic, but hardly as solely incapacitating."[79] Rather than reducing neuroscientific evidence to "two dimensions only – either benefiting or harming the defendant" – the system uses both rehabilitative *and* medical security measures. This approach protects society and a vulnerable defendant's needs.[80]

Would Slovenia's solution work in other countries, such as the substantially more punitive U.S.? The answer is unclear. Hafner stresses the concept of "Slovenian Exceptionalism" because of the country's low levels of crime and violence and a correctional system that endorses the rehabilitative use of neuroscientific evidence for vulnerable defendants.[81] Perhaps it's enough to say right now that the Slovenian system is well worth investigating. Morally and pragmatically, Slovenia has side-stepped the problem of the double-edged sword and the potentially devastating consequences for vulnerable defendants that can result from it.

1.6 Conclusion

"Vulnerable defendants," a broad and amorphous term, encapsulates individuals with a range of cognitive and learning disabilities that characterise a substantial portion of the prison population in most countries. The continuing growth of neuroscience in the courtroom and expanding alternatives to punishment increase opportunities to treat vulnerable defendants more fairly and adequately. Of course, using neuroscientific evidence creates risks and limitations, such as the double-edged sword concept. Yet, by examining how legal systems operate worldwide, we

---

78 Ibid 240-41.
79 Ibid 242.
80 Ibid.
81 Ibid 243.

come closer to developing a criminal justice system that protects both society and its most vulnerable members.

Acknowledgements

I am most grateful to Megan Martucci, Erica Valencia-Graham, Hannah Wishart, and Colleen Berryessa for their immensely helpful comments and contributions and to reference librarian Kathleen Thompson for her excellent research. I am indebted to six sources for research funding: Fordham University School of Law, Fordham's Neuroscience and Law Center, Mr. and Mrs. John R. Costantino, the Gerald M. Edelman Post-Graduate Fellowship in Neuroscience, the Roger Sachs Family Foundation, and the Barnet and Sharon Phillips Family Fund. No individual or organisation acknowledged in this chapter necessarily supports the chapter's interpretations or conclusions. I take responsibility for any mistakes or misjudgments.

2 Offering Neurotechnology to Defendants

On Vulnerability, Voluntariness, and Consent

Sjors Ligthart and Gerben Meynen

2.1 Introduction

In recent years, we have witnessed substantial progress in the field of neurotechnology. Generally, these technologies are of two kinds: they either aim to *obtain* information from the brain or *change* the brain – and sometimes, these features are combined within one device.[1] These neurotechnologies are used primarily in healthcare but are also considered regarding education and the military. In the future, neurotechnologies may also be increasingly applied in criminal justice.

Some neurotechnologies are already used in legal practice today.[2] For example, neuroimaging can be useful in diagnosing brain disorders, such as epilepsy and certain forms of dementia, which may be helpful in evaluations of insanity.[3] Furthermore, some studies suggest that brain scans could contribute to the prediction of future dangerousness for convicted offenders.[4] Brain-derived data has also enabled researchers to make inferences about individual mental states, such as identifying whether a person has lied about certain facts.[5] This type of data may be useful in answering central questions in criminal law, such as whether a

---

1 For instance, closed-loop deep brain stimulation; S. Ligthart et al., "Closed-Loop Brain Devices in Offender Rehabilitation" (2021) 30 *Cambridge Quarterly Healthcare Ethics* 669. See also P.R. Roelfsema, D. Denys & P.C. Klink, "Mind Reading and Writing: The Future of Neurotechnology" (2018) 22 *Trends Cogn Sci* 598. Several techniques mentioned below are 'emerging' technologies still in the experimental phase.

2 D.W. Denno, this volume.

3 G. Meynen, "Neuroscience-based Psychiatric Assessments of Criminal Responsibility: Beyond self-report?" (2020) 29 *CQHE*, 446; J.R. Simpson (ed.), *Neuroimaging in Forensic Psychiatry* (Wiley-Blackwell 2012).

4 C. Delfin et al., "Prediction of recidivism in a long-term follow-up of forensic psychiatric patients" (2019) PLoS ONE doi.org/10.1371/journal.pone.0217127; E. Aharoni et al., "Neuroprediction of future rearrest" (2013) 110 *Proceedings of the National Acad Science* 6223.

5 E.H. Meijer et al., "Memory detection with the Concealed Information Test: A meta-analysis of skin conductance, respiration heart rate and P300 data" (2014) 51 *Psychophysiology*

DOI: 10.4324/9781003331056-3

person is guilty of a crime and should be held responsible. Furthermore, research suggests that altering and modifying the brain through neuro-interventions may reduce recidivism in convicted offenders.[6] For example, a recent study found that transcranial direct current stimulation (tDCS) reduced self-reported aggression in a forensic population.[7]

Employing sometimes far-reaching neurotechnologies in criminal justice without valid informed consent is likely to infringe a variety of fundamental rights, such as the right to privacy, bodily and mental integrity, and freedom of expression. Consequently, obtaining valid informed consent is crucial. There is a debate, however, about the legal and moral permissibility of offering neurotechnology to defendants and convicted offenders. For example, suppose a defendant was offered treatment with a form of neurotechnology as a condition for probation or lower sentences. In that case, this may raise concerns about the coerciveness and voluntariness – and therefore validity – of a defendant's consent to such an offer.[8] Due to the situational *vulnerability* of defendants – arising from the very nature of their position in criminal justice to which power asymmetry and dependency are inherent – offers as these may sometimes constitute as "an offer you cannot refuse."[9]

In addition, some defendants may be vulnerable because of their mental condition. For instance, a recent study found that "mental disorder[s] [were] more common in those attending court from custody, with 48.5% having at least one psychiatric diagnosis compared with 20.3% from the community."[10] Brown et al. have concluded:

> "[t]he prevalence of mental illness and neurodevelopmental disorders in defendants is high. Many are at risk of being unfit to plead and

879; J.P. Rosenfeld (ed.), *Detecting Concealed Information and Deception: Recent Developments* (Academic Press, 2018).

6 N.A. Vincent, T. Nadelhoffer & A. McCay (eds.), *Neurointerventions and the Law: Regulating Human Mental Capacity* (Oxford University Press, New York 2020).

7 C.S. Sergiou et al., "Transcranial Direct Current Stimulation Targeting the Ventromedial Prefrontal Cortex Reduces Reactive Aggression and Modulates Electrophysiological Responses in a Forensic Population" (2022) 7 *Biol Psychiatry Cogn Neurosci Neuroimaging*: CNNI 95. Cf. J. Fuss et al., "Deep brain stimulation to reduce sexual drive", (2015) 40 *Journal of Psychiatry Neuroscience* 429.

8 J. Pugh, "Coercion and the Neurocorrective Offer" in D. Birks & T. Douglas (eds.), *Treatment for Crime* (OUP 2018); J. Ryberg, *Neurointerventions, Crime, and Punishment* (Oxford University Press, New York, 2020); S. Ligthart, *Coercive Brain-Reading in Criminal Law* (Cambridge University Press, 2022).

9 P. Kellmeyer, N. Biller-Andorno & G. Meynen, "Ethical tensions of virtual reality treatment in vulnerable patients" (2019) 25 *Nat. Med.* 1185; G. Meynen, "Brain-based Mind Reading in Forensic Psychiatry" (2017) 4 *Journal of Law and Biosciences* 311.

10 P. Brown et al., "Prevalence of mental disorders in defendants at criminal court" (2022) 8 *BJPsych Open* 1.

require additional support at court, yet are not identified by existing services. Our evidence challenges policymakers and healthcare providers to ensure that vulnerable defendants are adequately supported at court."[11]

In fact, this means that some "double vulnerability" exists in a considerable percentage of defendants.[12] While the first type of vulnerability can be considered *situational*, the second is more *pathogenic*.[13] Although both types of vulnerability are relevant in this chapter, the emphasis will be on the situational type.[14]

In what follows, we explore the relevance of a defendant's vulnerability to the validity of consent to a neurotechnology offer within criminal justice contexts. The approach is primarily legal, focusing on the European Convention on Human Rights (ECHR). Although this chapter emphasises defendants, some arguments may also apply to offering neurotechnology to convicted offenders.[15]

2.2 Vulnerability and the Validity of Consent

Different strategies and levels of pressure can be used to get others to act as you wish, such as persuasion, leverage, making offers, exploitation, manipulation, making threats, and employing physical force.[16] Not all such means attain "coercion". The relevance of identifying what constitutes coercion and what does not lies in the widely accepted view that coercion is incompatible with valid consent.[17] Generally, valid consent requires (1) the disclosure of appropriate information, (2) that the person is competent, and (3) that he or she is permitted to make

11 Brown et al. 2022.

12 O. Choy, F. Focquaert & A. Raine, "Benign Biological Interventions to Reduce Offending" (2020) 13 *Neuroethics* 29.

13 See classification by C. Mackenzie, W. Rogers & S. Dodds, *Vulnerability: New Essays in Ethics and Feminist Philosophy* (Oxford University Press, New York, 2013) and Kellmeyer, Biller-Andorno & Meynen 2019.

14 Generally, the concerns regarding vulnerability we discuss in this chapter may also be relevant to *research* on neurotechnology in defendants, but we will focus on actual offering neurotechnology in criminal justice practices. See G. Meynen, "Walls and Laws: Structural Barriers to Forensic Psychiatric Research" (2017) 44 *European Psychiatry* 208.

15 See S. Ligthart, E. Dore-Horgan & G. Meynen, 'The Various Faces of Vulnerability: Offering Neurointerventions to Criminal Offenders', (2023) 10 *Journal of Law and the Biosciences* 1

16 J. Feinberg, *The Moral Limits of the Criminal Law: Volume 3: Harm to Self* (OUP 1989), 189; G. Szmukler & P.S. Appelbaum, "Treatment pressures, leverage, coercion, and compulsion in mental health care", (2008) 17 *Journal of Mental Health* 2008 233.

17 M. Kiener, 'Coercion', in E. Craig (ed.), *Routledge Encyclopedia of Philosophy* (Version 2, 2020), sect. 5; N. Eyal, 'Informed Consent', in E.N. Zalta (ed.), *The Stanford Encyclopedia of Philosophy* (Spring 2019 Edition), sect. 5.1.

a voluntary choice.[18] Coercion impairs *voluntariness* and, therefore, invalidates consent.[19] In philosophy, some theorists accept that making a specific offer to a person in a vulnerable situation could amount to coercion and render consent invalid.[20] In the law, too, courts and scholars have considered the vulnerability of defendants and convicted offenders as a relevant factor for determining voluntariness and, thus, the validity of informed consent.[21]

The concept of informed consent is, among others, relevant to the protection offered by human rights. Valid consent can prevent infringements of human rights, for example, in the context of surgery or in the course of police powers, such as searching cars and homes.[22] Often, discussions on consent and human rights relate to medical interventions in criminal justice, such as forced feeding in prison,[23] surgical castration of sex offenders,[24] and gynaecological examination of female prisoners.[25] When valid consent exists for medical procedure, such as is often the case in medicine, human rights will not typically be infringed. The European Court on Human Rights (ECtHR) has endorsed this view. For example, in the case of *Bogumil/Portugal*, a swallowed package of cocaine had been surgically removed from the suspect's stomach (for safety reasons). There was insufficient evidence to establish that the suspect had given his consent or that he had refused and had been forced to undergo the operation. Yet, the ECtHR considered that if the suspect had given informed consent to this medical procedure, no issue would have arisen under the prohibition of ill-treatment under Article 3 ECHR.[26] In *Pretty/UK*, the Court stressed that medical interventions *without* the consent of a mentally competent patient will infringe the right to physical integrity under Article 8 ECHR.[27]

18 Eyal 2019, sect. 1; R. Faden, T.L. Beauchamp & N.M.P. King, *A History and Theory of Informed Consent* (Oxford University Press, New York, 1986).
19 S. Anderson, 'Coercion', in E.N. Zalte (ed.), *The Stanford Encyclopedia of Philosophy* (Summer 2021 Edition), sect. 3.3; Faden, Beauchamp & King 1986, Ch. 7 and 10.
20 E.g., J. McGregor, 'Undue Influence as Coercive Offers in Clinical Trials' in D.A. Reify & W.J. Riker (eds.), *Coercion and the State* (Springer, 2008).
21 E.g., W. Buelens, C. Herijgers & S. Illegems, "The View of the European Court of Human Rights on Competent Patients' Right of Informed Consent" (2016) 23 *European Journal of Health Law*, 481; Ligthart 2022.
22 D.J. Harris et al., *Harris, O'Boyle, and Warbrick: Law of the European Convention on Human Rights* (Oxford University Press, Oxford, 2018), 238.
23 P. Jacobs, *Force-feeding of prisoners and detainees on hunger strike* (Intersentia 2012), 68–72.
24 CPT/Inf (2012) 6, point 145.
25 *Juhnke/Turkey*, ECtHR 13 May 2008, 52515/99; *Y.F./Turkey*, ECtHR 22 July 2003, 24209/94.
26 *Bogumil/Portugal*, ECtHR 3 October 2008, 35228/03, 71.
27 *Pretty/UK*, ECtHR 29 April 2002, 2346/02, at 63.

A defendant's vulnerability seems exceedingly relevant to the concept of consent. At present, however, in-depth debates on theoretical understandings of vulnerability, consent, and coercion seem to have had little central concern in common legal scholarship.[28] Under the ECHR, for example, no generic legal account on coercion has yet been developed.[29] In philosophy, however, coercion and consent have received considerable attention;[30] thus, section 2.2.1 will provide a brief descriptive account of the philosophical conceptualisation of coercion, consent, and vulnerability. We will not take a position in the philosophical debate. Instead, we intend to outline the contours of a conceptual framework that can help to better understand case law presided by the European Court on Human Rights (ECtHR). The ECtHR's position will be discussed in section 2.2.2.

2.2.1 *The Philosophical Debate*

As Kiener writes, coercion comes in two types: physical and volitional coercion.[31] *Physical* coercion works through employing direct force, determining – often restricting – a person's movements. For example, suppose you are pushing someone against the wall, handcuffing, or imprisoning a person. That would qualify as physical coercion. Regarding the enforcement of neurotechnologies, physical coercion will however often be ineffective, as most of these technologies require cooperation of the subject, such as attentively observing presented stimuli, performing a cognitive task, or sitting tight without generating brain activity that could complicate the neurotechnological procedure.[32] Employing physical force to effectuate this kind of cooperation is hard to imagine.

Unlike physical coercion, *volitional* coercion usually works through making threats and arranging a person's situation so that he or she is compelled to perform a certain act to avoid harm.[33] A paradigmatic example is a robber's threat, "Your money or your life!" This threat arranges another person's situation so that he or she has no choice but to hand

---

28 Some examples: G. Lamond, "The coerciveness of Law" (2000) 20 *Oxford Journal of Legal Studies* 39; R.C. Hughes, "Law and Coercion" (2013) 8 *Philosophy Compass* 231; Cf. A. Wertheimer, *Coercion* (Princeton University Press, 1987), which approach has been developed and defended in US legal reasoning.

29 Ligthart 2022.

30 For an overview see Kiener 2020; Anderson 2021.

31 Kiener 2020, sect. 1; Anderson 2021, sect. 2.1.1.

32 Ligthart 2022. Think, for example, of the detection of recognition, lie detection or neuroprediction with functional neuroimaging, which all require the subject to observe certain stimuli and/or perform a certain task, such as pressing a yes-or-no button.

33 Kiener 2020, sect. 1; Anderson 2021, sect. 2.2.

over the money to avoid being killed. Whereas it is generally accepted that *threats* coerce, there is an ongoing debate about whether *offers* can sometimes also be coercive. Some theorists argue that only threats coerce,[34] while others contend that offers could also amount to coercion in some instances, often referred to as "coercive offers."[35] In short, the distinction between threats and offers is that threats make recipients worse off, while offers make them better off.[36] The abovementioned robber's proposal – "Hand over your money, or I will kill you"– typically qualifies as a threat, as the robber creates a situation in which the prospect of being killed leaves little choice for the individual being compelled to hand over his or her money. An offer could be "If you pay me, I will treat your broken leg," as a treatment option is suddenly created that will make a person better off. Unlike threats, offers will not normally restrict the recipient's freedom and are, thus, not normally considered coercive.

Yet it has been argued that proposals could also coerce if there is a "coercive offer."[37] There are different reasons why some theorists argue that offers could, sometimes, amount to coercion. One of them relates to the *situational vulnerability* of the recipient. For example, McGregor writes:

> Getting the Congolese prisoner who is fed only twice a week by the warden to participate in a nontherapeutic and risky medical trial does not require the threat of harm if he fails to participate. The offer of four meals a week in exchange to agreeing to participate would suffice. People in miserable, vulnerable situations can be influenced, induced, "forced" with minor offers, to do all kinds of things. Would it be a fully voluntary choice to participate in research in the Congolese prisoner example?[38]

According to McGregor, offers can coerce if they are the only eligible option for the recipient in a miserable or vulnerable situation. Typically, offers make their recipients "better off" compared to the normal course of

---

34 E.g. Wertheimer 1987; R. Nozick, 'Coercion', in S. Morgenbesser, P. Suppes, & M. White (eds.), *Philosophy, Science, and Method Essays in Honor of Ernest Nagel*, (St. Martin's Press, Toronto, 1969), 440.

35 Feinberg 1989; McGregor 2008;

36 Kiener 2020, sect. 2; Anderson 2021, sect. 2.2. Determining whether a proposal makes someone worse off, qualifying as a threat, requires a certain baseline, i.e., a hypothetical situation to compare with the situation after the proposer's intervention. Two baselines are to be distinguished: a statistical baseline (the normally expected course of events), and a moral baseline (the morally required course of events).

37 Feinberg 1989, p. 229.

38 McGregor 2008, p. 52.

events. However, if the recipient finds herself in miserable circumstances with no other options left, and the proposer takes advantage of that situation, offers can have similar effects as threats.[39] As McGregor emphasises, the more miserable a person's situation is, the easier it is to "offer" a better situation and get that person to do what you want. If only threats were coercive, the most worse off and most vulnerable people would be the hardest to coerce, since making them worse off is difficult. However, disadvantaged, vulnerable populations should be considered more susceptible to coercion, not less so.[40] In McGregor's view, for an offer to be coercive, it is relevant whether the weaker party is dependent in some way on the stronger party and whether the stronger party has influence over whether some significant evil occurs (or continues) to the weaker party. If the stronger party takes advantage of this power imbalance by offering a worse deal than he or she would do otherwise, this offer then qualifies as coercion.[41] The imbalance of power also seems relevant to Zimmerman's perspective on coercion, as he writes:

> If P throws Q into the water and then offers to save Q (where he can do so at relatively little cost to himself) only if Q promises to give him his life savings afterwards, the offer is coercive and the promise void. If P just happens upon the scene, sees Q drowning, and offers to rescue him on exactly the same terms, Q's promise is probably just as void, morally speaking anyway, since P's offer is so grossly exploitive. But it does not follow from just this that P has coerced Q.[42]

In considering whether offers could coerce, Zimmerman argues, we should take into account whether the proposer *controls or arranges* the recipient's original situation.[43] The coerciveness of offers is a much-debated topic. Yet, despite the morally appealing idea that a person's vulnerability could somehow adversely affect voluntariness or otherwise invalidate consent, many scholars reject the existence of coercive offers.[44]

Interestingly, apart from coercion, other forms of external pressure could also adversely affect voluntariness and consent. Faden, Beauchamp, and King argue that sometimes, controlling influences fall short of

39 Ibid.
40 Ibid.
41 Ibid, p. 54. Cf. the distinctive concept of "exploitation"; Feinberg 1989, p. 245 et seq.
42 D. Zimmerman, 'Coercive Wage Offers', (1981) 10 *Philosophy & Public Affairs* 121, 134–135.
43 Preventing the recipient from moving from the actual pre-proposal situation to some alternative, more preferable pre-proposal situation. Idem, p. 132–136.
44 E.g., A. Wertheimer & F.G. Miller, 'There are (STILL) no coercive offers' (2014) 40 *Journal of Medical Ethics*, Anderson 2021, sect. 2.4.

coercion but can still restrict autonomy and invalidate consent.[45] In such "in between" cases, the exerted pressure could qualify as "manipulation",[46] which they define as follows:

> *Manipulation* is a catch-all category that includes any intentional and successful influence of a person by noncoercively altering the actual choices available to the person or by nonpersuasively altering the person's perceptions of those choices. The essence of manipulation is getting people to do what the manipulator intends by one of these two general means.[47]

Different types of manipulative influences are conceivable. One of them concerns the *manipulation of options*, involving direct modification of the options available to an individual to alter his behaviour or beliefs.[48] For example, manipulators can decrease or increase the number of options, or even reward their preferred behaviour. Often, these methods are employed together: "The manipulator simultaneously creates a new option such as the 'opportunity' to participate in research or to receive a new medical treatment, and gerrymanders the reward structure so that the option presented is clearly preferable."[49] In this regard, power asymmetry and a person's vulnerability could be relevant, or even crucial, factors. As Noggle writes:

> The idea that manipulation can be a tool for the powerful to oppress the less powerful is not new (…) A relative lack of socio-political power is almost certainly one source of vulnerability to manipulation. But there are likely others as well. The trickery model of manipulation suggests—plausibly—that people who are less intellectually sophisticated are especially vulnerable to trickery and therefore to manipulation. The pressure model suggests that financial, social, and emotional desperation may make one especially vulnerable to pressures created by threats to worsen an already tenuous situation.[50]

In medical ethics, it is widely accepted that apart from coercion, some forms of manipulation interfere with autonomous decision-making and

---

45 Faden, Beauchamp & King 1986, 259.
46 See also R. Noggle, 'The Ethics of Manipulation', in E.N. Zalta (ed.), *The Stanford Encyclopedia of Philosophy* (Summer 2020 Edition), sect. 2.3.
47 Faden, Beauchamp & King 1986, p. 261. Cf. Feinberg 1989, p. 189.
48 Faden, Beauchamp & King 1986, p. 355.
49 Ibid.
50 Noggle 2020, sect. 4.3

invalidate informed consent.[51] The potential coerciveness, or otherwise involuntariness, of consent to specific criminal justice offers has received considerable attention in practical ethics. An example is offering convicted sex offenders early release from prison if they consent to surgical or chemical castration.[52] We can imagine similar offers to defendants as well. Consider, for instance, offering a defendant the ability to avoid a prison sentence if he or she consents to continuous monitoring using neurotechnology. Other examples are the offer to reduce sentences if one consents to a neurointervention that aims to reduce the risk of recidivism[53] or the offer to undergo neuroimaging as a condition for bail or probation.[54]

2.2.2 A Legal Perspective

Yet, no systematic theory about coercion and consent has been developed under the ECHR.[55] For example, regarding criminal suspects and the privilege against self-incrimination, the ECtHR refrains from providing a central approach on which types and degrees of pressure are acceptable and which are not.[56] Meanwhile, case law cautiously suggests the tentative contours of an implicit approach to different kinds of pressure with informed consent to State interferences. At least, it seems to indicate that apart from direct threats, other means of influencing vulnerable people's decision-making could also invalidate consent.[57]

First, it is clear that *threatening* to enforce cooperation with governmental investigations invalidates the voluntariness of consent and raises an issue under the human rights that apply to a particular case. For example, under Article 8 ECHR, the Court considers:

> that the taking of a DNA sample from the applicant amounted to an interference with his 'private life' within the meaning of Article 8 of the Convention. The fact that the applicant agreed to give a sample

---

51 Ibid, sect. 1.2 and 3.3.
52 J. McMillan, "The kindest cut?" (2014) 40 *J. Med. Ethics* 583;Wertheimer & Miller 2014; T. Douglas et al., "Coercion, Incarceration, and Chemical Castration", (2013) 10 *Journal of Bioethical Inquiry* 393.
53 Ryberg 2020, Ch. 2; Pugh 2018; F. Focquaert, K. Van Assche & S. Sterckx "Offering Neurointerventions to Offenders With Cognitive-Emotional Impairments" in Vincent, Nadelhoffer & McCay 2020.
54 Meynen 2017; Ligthart 2022.
55 Ligthart 2022, Ch. 8; G. Richardson, "Coercion and human rights", (2008) 17 *Journal of Mental Health* 245.
56 *John Murray/UK*, ECtHR 8 February 1996, 18731/91, 46.
57 Ligthart 2022, Ch. 8.

of his saliva to the police officers was, in this context, of no relevance, since he only did so under the threat that either a saliva sample or a blood sample would otherwise be taken from him by force.[58]

Other examples from the case law concern threats to participate in X-rays for tuberculosis screening (non-compliance was punishable),[59] as well as threats to provide a urine sample for drug testing in prison (refusal was threatened with disciplinary sanctions and additional days of detention).[60]

Second, the ECtHR seems to accept that more *subtle means of indirect pressure* could impair voluntariness by invalidating consent and raising issues under the human rights in question. At least, the very nature of criminal justice – either during police investigation,[61] at trial,[62] or in prison[63] – involves an imbalance of power and, therefore, constitutes a certain level of vulnerability on the part of suspects and convicted offenders, which requires critical scrutiny of the voluntariness of their consenting decisions.[64]

For example, in *R.S./Hungary*, the applicant complained about a violation of Article 3 ECHR (prohibition of ill-treatment), as he had been catheterised under the control of police officers to determine whether he was under the influence of alcohol or drugs as a road user. Concerning the validity of the applicant's consent, the Court had "doubts as to whether the applicant, being in the hands of the authorities and in their complete control, had any option in practice but to undergo the impugned procedure."[65] A similar reasoning has been adopted in gynaecological examinations involving female detainees in Turkish prisons. For instance, in *Juhnke/Turkey*, the applicant complained that she had been subjected to a gynaecological examination without valid consent during her imprisonment.[66] The Turkish government argued that the examination aimed

---

58 *Dragan Petrović/Serbia*, ECtHR 14 April 2020, 75229/10, 79.

59 EComHR 10 December 1984, appl.no. 10435/83 (*Acmanne and others/Belgium*).

60 EComHR 6 April 1994, appl.no. 21132/93 (*Peters/The Netherlands*); EComHR 9 September 1998, appl.no. 34199/96 (*Galloway/UK*); ECtHR 11 October 2005, appl.no. 60682/00 (*Young/UK*).

61 *Panovits/Cyprus*, ECtHR 11 December 2008, 4268/04, 68; *R.S./Hungary*, ECtHR 2 July 2019, 65290/14, 65.

62 *John Murray/UK*, ECtHR 8 February 1996, 18731/91, 49–50; *Averill/UK*, ECtHR 6 June 2000, 36408/97, 48.

63 *Juhnke/Turkey*, ECtHR 13 May 2008, appl.no. 52515/99, 76; *Yazgül Yılmaz/Turkey*, ECtHR 1 February 2011, 36369/06, 45.

64 Cf. Buelens, Herijgers & Illegems 2016, 484–485; K. de Vries, 'Right to Respect for Private and Family Life', in P. van Dijk et al. (eds.), *Theory and Practice of the European Convention on Human Rights* (Intersentia 2018), 667, 694.

65 *R.S./Hungary*, ECtHR 2 July 2019, 65290/14, 65.

66 *Juhnke/Turkey*, ECtHR 13 May 2008, 52515/99.

to protect the prison guards from false allegations of rape and that the applicant had given consent to it.[67] Regarding the voluntariness of consent, the Court considered that:

> in certain circumstances, a person in detention cannot be expected to continue to resist submitting to a gynaecological examination, given her *vulnerability at the hands of the authorities*, who exercise *complete control* over her throughout her detention.[68]

The Court found a violation of the right to respect for private life under Article 8 ECHR.[69] Under Article 6 ECHR (the right to a fair trial), vulnerability and power asymmetry appear to be relevant factors in assessing a voluntary waiver's validity. In *Panovits/Cyprus*, the Court argued that:

> given the *vulnerability* of an accused minor and the *imbalance of power to which he is subjected by the very nature of criminal proceedings*, a waiver by him or on his behalf of an important right under Article 6 can only be accepted where it is expressed in an unequivocal manner after the authorities have taken all reasonable steps to ensure that he or she is fully aware of his rights of defence and can appreciate, as far as possible, the consequence of his conduct.[70]

Indirect pressure due to power asymmetry was also essential in the case of *Allan/UK*, where a cellmate informant was used to elicit incriminating statements from the applicant about murder. During the police interrogations, the applicant had invoked the right to remain silent. The Court emphasised that the right to remain silent and the privilege against self-incrimination serve, in principle, to protect the freedom of the accused to choose whether to speak or to remain silent when questioned by the police. This freedom, the Court continued, is not confined to cases of direct compulsion. Instead, the protected freedom of choice can also be effectively undermined when the authorities use subterfuge to elicit self-incriminating statements. In this case, the applicant had been:

> subjected to psychological pressures which impinged on the "voluntariness" of the disclosures allegedly made by the applicant to

---

67 Ibid, § 60.
68 *Juhnke/Turkey*, ECtHR 13 May 2008, 52515/99, 76 (emphasis added).
69 See also *Y.F./Turkey*, ECtHR 22 July 2003, 24209/94; *Yazgül Yılmaz/Turkey*, ECtHR 1 February 2011, 36369/06.
70 *Panovits/Cyprus*, ECtHR 11 December 2008, 4268/04, 68 (emphasis added).

H. [the informant]: he was a suspect in a murder case, in detention and under direct pressure from the police in interrogations about the murder, and would have been susceptible to persuasion to take H., with whom he shared a cell for some weeks, into his confidence.[71]

Although the authorities, in this case, did not use any physical coercion or legal threats, the psychological pressure that partly arose from detention and the criminal proceedings against the applicant likely adversely affected the voluntariness of the self-incriminating statements.[72] The Court argued that, in those circumstances, the evidence must be regarded as having been obtained in defiance of the applicant's will because its use at trial violated the right to silence and the privilege against self-incrimination.

As these examples illustrate, situational vulnerability and power asymmetry are relevant factors in determining the voluntariness of consent in case law. Yet it is unclear whether these factors could render an offer as *coercive* – as argued by McGregor and Zimmerman – or whether the ECtHR implicitly accepts a broader continuum of (non-coercive) influences that could impair voluntariness and invalidate consent, such as manipulation.

2.3 Discussion: The Relevance of Vulnerability

As discussed in the previous sections, there is an ongoing theoretical debate in philosophy about if and how vulnerability could be relevant to the validity of informed consent. In the case law of the ECtHR, vulnerability plays a role when determining the validity of consent in criminal justice contexts. However, no theoretical approach exists within the law regarding how different forms of vulnerability relate to informed consent, coercion, or, for example, manipulation. If neurotechnologies are increasingly offered to defendants, a coherent approach to informed consent and different forms of pressure will be valuable for human rights analyses. After all, the absence of valid consent to a neurotechnological application will often raise an infringement or even a violation of the person's fundamental human rights, such as the right to privacy and bodily and mental integrity.

Meanwhile, in our view, it is important to recognise that compelling reasons may sometimes exist to offer neurotechnologies to defendants, or at least not to withhold the choice to participate in neuroimaging or a brain intervention. Below, we briefly consider two arguments, which consecutively relate to (1) paternalism and (2) a possible right to neurotechnology.

---

71 *Allan/UK*, ECtHR 5 November 2002, 48539/99, 52.
72 Cf. J.D. Jackson & S.J. Summers, *The Internationalization of Criminal Evidence* (CUP 2012), 55–56.

Paternalism can be defined as "the interference of a state or an individual with another person, against their will, and defended or motivated by a claim that the person interfered with will be better off or protected from harm."[73] Preventing defendants from making their *own* decisions regarding accepting some form of neurotechnology – just because of their vulnerable position – can be considered outright paternalistic.[74] Even though paternalism may be defensible in some cases, it is often still regarded as problematic, as confirmed by the ECtHR.[75]

In principle, respecting a person's autonomy requires accepting that people make their own choices. As discussed, when a choice is a product of coercion or manipulation, which may (partly) arise from a person's vulnerability, autonomy will not be respected, the choice will be unfree, and consent, such as for brain interventions, will therefore be invalid. As such, a defendant's vulnerability could depend on the situation or context and provide a compelling argument against the offering of neurotechnology to a defendant. At the same time, we should be careful in using this argument too easily to categorically deny defendants their choice of whether they would prefer the application of neurotechnology, such as a neurointervention to reduce aggressiveness, or, say, serve a long prison sentence.[76] Categorically denying defendants the opportunity to choose neurotechnology as an alternative for pretrial detention or a criminal sentence could, in fact, even *increase* situational vulnerability,[77] with important choices related to one's freedom (bail, sentencing, parole) further restricted only because we feel that vulnerability could somehow adversely affect the validity of informed consent.

Therefore, we would be inclined to argue that using the vulnerability argument requires making clear (A) how, in a particular case, vulnerability could nullify the validity of consent and (B) that the defendant in question

---

73 G. Dworkin, "Paternalism", in Z.N. Edward, *Stanford Encyclopedia of Philosophy* (Fall 2020 Edition).

74 On vulnerability, paternalism and denying prisoners the opportunity to participate in medical research, see L. Pasquerella, "Confining choices: should inmates' participation in research be limited?" (2002) 23 *Theor Med and Bioeth* 519. She writes about the U.S. context, among others: "twenty-two states have taken further steps to ban the use of inmates in biomedical research altogether. While these paternalistic measures are designed to protect a population that is vulnerable due to their environment from the abuses of the past, the effect in many instances has been to deny prisoners access to the only available treatment for their diseases."

75 *V.C./Slovakia*, ECtHR 8 November 2011, 18968/07, 114. Cf. *Jehovah's Witnesses of Moscow/Russia*, ECtHR 10 June 2010, 302/02, at 136.

76 Cf. L. Singh, "Making Progress in the Ethics of Digital and Virtual Technologies for Mental Health", (2022) 13 *AJOB-N*, 141; M.J. Blitz, "Extended Reality, Mental Liberty, and State Power in Forensic Settings", (2022) 13 *AJOB-N*, 173.

77 See also Choy, Focquaert & Raine 2020, p. 33.

is indeed vulnerable in a relevant way. In other words, we should be careful in always accepting vulnerability as a conclusive argument against neurotechnology offers because this may entail a problematic form of paternalism and deny defendants to make their own choices.

Secondly, one could argue that defendants also have a limited right to be offered neurotechnology.[78] As previously mentioned, the prevalence of mental illnesses and neurodevelopmental disorders in defendants is high; thus, this increases the risk of them being deemed unfit to plead at trial or fit to plead only with additional support, such as adaptive measures (e.g., a severe psychotic illness may lead to unfitness to stand trial, and antipsychotic medication may help to restore the defendant's mental capacities). Meanwhile, as Brown et al. state, these defendants may not always be identified by existing services.[79] Yet, policymakers and healthcare providers should ensure that vulnerable defendants are adequately supported in their criminal trials.[80] In principle, now or in the near future, certain types of neuroimaging could help to *identify* those who need such support. In addition, some neurointerventions could *support* some of those with mental illnesses and enable them to better represent their interests. In fact, one could argue that the State has a duty to offer potentially helpful technologies to those in vulnerable positions. For example, regarding vulnerable persons who suffer from mental disabilities, the official Guide on Article 8 ECHR notes:

> With regard to the positive obligations that Member States have in respect of vulnerable individuals suffering from mental illness, the Court has affirmed that mental health must also be regarded as a crucial part of private life associated with the aspect of moral integrity. The preservation of mental stability is in that context an indispensable precondition to effective enjoyment of the right to respect for private life.[81]

78 Cf. E. Dore-Horgan, "Do criminal offenders have a right to neurorehabilitation?", (2022) *Crim Law Philos*
       1, doi:10.1007/s11572-022-09630-y; J.C. Bublitz, 'Cognitive Liberty or the International Human Right to Freedom of Thought', in J. Clausen & N. Levy (eds.), *Handbook of Neuroethics*, (Springer Science 2015), 1309, 1317; Blitz 2022.
79 Brown et al. 2022 write: "There is international concern that large numbers of vulnerable defendants are not identified and are unfairly facing trials that they cannot fully participate in." Brown et al. themselves estimate based on empirical data that a considerable percentage of those who are, actually, unfit, are not identified as such in the criminal justice system.
80 Brown et al. 2022.
81 *Guide on Article 8 of the European Convention on Human Rights*, August 2021, 129.

If neurotechnology proves to be safe and effective in preserving the mental stability of vulnerable defendants – and, after conviction, of vulnerable convicted offenders – a positive obligation may exist for the State to offer these technologies.[82] Positive obligations in criminal justice have already been recognised, especially regarding the vulnerable group of criminal offenders. For example, under the prohibition of ill-treatment of Article 3 ECHR, the ECtHR holds that, in some cases, providing life prisoners with a real opportunity to rehabilitate themselves may require that "they be enabled to undergo treatments or therapies – be they medical, psychological or psychiatric – adapted to their situation with a view to facilitating their rehabilitation."[83] And from the right to liberty under Article 5 ECHR, the Court has argued that when detention is predominantly justified on the grounds of dangerousness and public protection, prisoners should be offered real opportunities for rehabilitation and to make progress through the prison system and become eligible for parole, such as by offering suitable therapy.[84]

2.4 Conclusion

In philosophy and law, obtaining a person's consent to potentially right-infringing State interferences is often crucial. This is particularly true for far-reaching procedures – such as neurotechnological interventions that aim to obtain brain information or modify neural features. Today, the use of neurotechnologies in criminal justice is quite rare. Yet, in the future, neurotechniques may become more prevalent in criminal justice, given recent developments in neuroscience. In this chapter, we have problematised the validity of a defendant's consent to neurotechnology based on his or her vulnerability. We have shown that both philosophy and law suggest that choices made in vulnerable situations may sometimes invalidate consent for State interference. From this perspective, a defendant's vulnerability could be a persuasive argument against offering neurotechnologies to defendants in criminal justice contexts.

Meanwhile, we also caution against the categorical use or application of this argument. First, too much emphasis on vulnerability in this sense could, in practice, lead to paternalism, which may deprive defendants of the possibility to make their own choices about something of great

---

82 Cf. Dore-Horgan 2022; J. Rueda & E. Dore-Horgan, "A Virtual Prosthesis for Morality?", (2022) 13 *AJOB-N*, 163.

83 *Murray/The Netherlands*, ECtHR 26 April 2016, 10511/10, at 109.

84 *Sy/Italy*, ECtHR 24 January 2022, 11791/20; *Klinkenbuß/Germany*, ECtHR 25 February 2016, 53157/11, at 47; *James, Wells en Lee/UK*, ECtHR 18 September 2012, 25119/09, 57715/09 and 57877/09, at 217–218.

value: their freedom. Moreover, in-principle denying defendants to make such important decisions themselves could even increase their situational vulnerability since options to escape pretrial detection or imprisonment by accepting, for example, neurotechnological monitoring, may be taken away from them. Secondly, defendants may face both situational and pathogenic vulnerability because of mental illness. Neurotechnologies could help detect cognitive challenges resulting from these illnesses and support defendants during criminal trials – a phase in which people often must make hard choices with deep impacts on their lives. In this respect, we suggest that defendants might also have a right to the available neurotechnological options to preserve or restore their mental stability and reduce vulnerability. Exploring the moral foundations, legal justifications, and tentative contours of such a positive right to neurotechnology in criminal justice would, in our view, be conducive to the ongoing debate on neurotechnology, law, and vulnerable people.

Acknowledgements

This publication is part of the project Law and Ethics of Neuroethologies in Criminal Justice, which is funded by the Dutch Research Council (NWO; VI.C.201.067).

3 Vulnerable Defendants

Redefining Decision-Making through the Lenses of Neuroscience, Law and Artificial Intelligence

Amedeo Santosuosso and Matilde Giustiniani

3.1 Introduction: Obverting the Conversation on Neuroscience and Law

The following contribution raises an important, and less discussed, issue at the nexus of neuroscience and law that is becoming increasingly critical with the advent of AI . Specifically, advances in AI may challenge the pillars of our justice system through the lenses of neuroscientific discoveries and lead to questions about the values and forces we want our social system to uphold.

In the past several decades, neuroscience has become a more common form of evidence to aid in contextualising the mental capacity, and thus, potential understandings of culpability and accountability, of vulnerable defendants. We define vulnerable defendants as any person under 18 years old or whose ability to participate in a trial is affected by a mental or physical disorder or an impairment of their intellectual or social functioning.[1] In this sense, neuroscience has begun to reshape our understanding of human decision-making by giving way to longstanding debates on the interactions between impulse and reason and their roles or impact in evaluating a defendant's culpability. For example, in the *Mattiello* case, in Italy,[2] neuroscientific evaluations of the defendant were used to support an insanity defence. However, advancements in neuroscience have not yet reached deeper cores of legal systems – with still little understanding of how the rationality and decision-making of the pillars of the justice system, i.e. judges and lawyers, can be compromised by neuroscience. This harms the notion of a transparent and reliable legal system. Despite resistance to change from the judiciary,

---

1 P. Cooper, J. Grace, 'Vulnerable Patients Going to Court: A Psychiatrist's Guide to Special Measures' (2016) 40 *BJPsych Bulletin* 220.
2 O. D. Jones, J. D. Schall, F. X. Shen, *Law and Neuroscience* (2 edn, Aspen Publishing 2020) 14.

DOI: 10.4324/9781003331056-4

the emergence of new intelligent machines capable of interacting with decision-making within the Italian justice system may help allow neuroscience to be effectively considered in criminal processes – allowing for progress towards more mindful and humane decisions in cases involving vulnerable defendants.

This chapter intends to begin a new conversation about how neuroscience can be inserted into decision-making generally and in cases involving vulnerable defendants in the legal system. In section 3.2, we will discuss the nature of decision-making for vulnerable defendants within the Italian legal system by focusing on the principles that currently govern the notion of due process of law and the challenges that human behaviour can create for decision-making. The third section thoroughly discusses these challenges of what it means to be human and to make decisions. We address misconceptions that characterise the interactions between cognition and emotion and how they might influence decision-making of vulnerable defendants within the legal system, highlighting how these interactions may demand a revised conception of legal rationality. In the fourth section, we introduce the element of empathy and the role it plays in our relationships with and to one another, discussing, in particular, how such feelings are often very prejudiced choices in favour of those who are similar to us and may be especially stringent when we are confronted with cases involving vulnerable defendants.

Finally, based on the prior sections, we address how decision-makers should potentially reflect and weigh neuroscience in decision-making in cases involving vulnerable defendants. We particularly focus on the capacity of AI and new "intelligent machines" to provide more objective guidelines for decisions potential in such decisions. We want to clarify that the chapter in no way poses to be a thorough analysis of the complex confluence of neuroscience, AI, and law. Rather it proposes to be a mere introduction to these issues by aiming to elicit interest in a much-overlooked new frontier deserving of future attention.

3.2 Legal Decision-Making and Due Process of Law

Legal systems in Western countries are largely inspired by the fundamental notion of "due process of law," which takes different forms and emphases in other jurisdictions but is in some ways universally shared in common and civil law countries. For example, in the U.S., the Fourteenth Amendment of the Bill of Rights establishes the grounds for the right to due process, granting the citizens protection against the government's deprivation of a person's fundamental rights to life, liberty, or property without due process of law. The notion of due process of law inscribes several basic axioms that provide the standards of procedural *fairness*.[3] A procedural process is considered fair if it follows the *audi alteram partem* principle, guaranteeing that both parties are fairly, properly and publicly heard. If it grants an independent and impartial tribunal, if the decision is founded solely on the proof and evidence provided by the parties, and if all decisions are clearly motivated.[4] In the Italian Constitution, Article 111 clearly states that all court trials must be conducted with adversarial proceedings and that parties are entitled to equal conditions before an impartial judge, and that this limits the power of the decision-maker to decide *ad libitum*, avoiding judicial subjectivism.[5] Among other principles that provide the pillars for due process of law, courts' impartiality, independence, and objectivity are necessary for a fair and just court.[6]

Adherence to impartiality establishes a requirement for rational decision-making on the part of the judge so that decision-making should be governed by rules and sequential reasoning (a concept often juxtaposed to that of data-driven decision-making of intelligent machines, which often results in the non-traceability of decisional steps, namely the black box effect). Indeed, according to legal doctrine, judicial decision-making is assumed to be an expression of rule-based decision-making – a decisional process primarily based on rules (i.e., legislation). Obedience to these rules should require a transparent and clear legal justification for decisions, thus, further ensuring the right of an opposing party to object to the decision or to understand the rules that underlie how the decision came to be. This is the type of decision-making afforded by due process of law.[7]

Rule-based decision-making is a complex field, not synonymous with decisions made legally. In its proper and strict sense, decision-making is the way of deciding according to a written, clearly defined rule; as Frederick Schauer, author of a fundamental study on playing by the rules, clearly states, "rule-governed decision-making is a subset of legal decision-making, rather than being congruent with it."[8] According to this very demanding definition, many decisions taken by

3 A. Giordano, 'Intelligenza Artificiale e Giusto Processo Civile,' *L'intelligenza artificiale tra scienza, etica e diritto* (Munera 2022) 113–124.
4 H. J. Friendly, 'Some Kind of Hearing' (1975) 123 *University of Pennsylvania Law Review* 1267.
5 M. Bove, 'Art. 111 Cost. e 'Giusto Processo Civile',' *Rivista di diritto processuale*, vol 57 (Associazione ESSPER periodici italiani di economia, scienze sociali e storia 2002) 490; L. Lanfranchi, 'Giusto Processo Nell'enciclopedia Treccani' (*Enciclopedia Giuridica Treccani* 2001) 9 <https://www.treccani.it/enciclopedia/giusto-processo> (accessed 2022).
6 Supra note. 5.
7 Ibid.
8 F. Schauer, *Playing by the Rules: A Philosophical Examination of Rule-Based Decision-Making in Law and in Life* (Clarendon Press, Oxford, 1991) p. 1.

a legitimately appointed court – according to more subjective criteria such as the "best interest" of the child or a medical patient or the unlimited or wide-ranging factors that can be considered in sentencing decisions – are all legal, but not rule-based, decisions. Indeed, as discussed here, non-rule-based factors are at the core of shaping most legal decisions.

The current model of legal decision-making, which withholds rights and protections stemming from due process, assumes impartiality and legal justification as achievable standards of decision-making and as a gold standard of conduct. It delineates the image of a rational human as being able to act and make decisions in accordance with legal rules and unaffected by outside social or behavioural influences. Moreover, this understanding must consider that law also does not entail clearly defined boundaries and, on the contrary, provides considerable room for interpretation.

Different approaches have been delineated in the legal theoretical tradition, questioning the meaning of "logic" within the law and advancing the idea that legal motivation might not be truthfully transparent. It can be sufficient to recall Oliver Wendell Holmes Jr., who opens his volume "The Common Law" with the provocative statement, "the life of the law has not been logic."[9] A non-rationalistic approach in law is given by the famous current of thought, namely judicial realism,[10] which advances the possibility that justifications, rather than tracing the decisional steps of legal circumstance *inter-operam*, are explanations elaborated *a-posteriori*. From this perspective, a legal decision-maker, such as a judge, justifies his choice after it has been made by tracing a thread of consistency from inputs to outputs and following the rules to his motivational needs. This consequently leads to decision-making that is more arbitrary and subjective.

However, legal theoretical tradition needs to be faster to understand how such factors can influence legal decision-making; in the legal setting, irrationality and emotions have remained curbed to a cultural provocation. Indeed, the conception of *mens rea* constitutes the psychological axiom of crime – establishing the state of rationality or full mental capacity as the standard of humans, from which any significant deviation can represent an excusing condition that can reduce or even exclude criminal responsibility. Justice juxtaposes the rational human, that is, the representative figures of the judge and lawyers, with the criminal as two opposing representatives of rationality and impulsivity. This perpetuates a

---

9 W.O. Holmes Jr, 'The Common Law 1881' Lecture I, p. 1.
10 K. Olivecrona, *Law as fact*, (Stevens & Sons, London, 1971); A. Ross. *On Law and Justice.* (Stevens & Sons, London, 1958), 1

conception of emotion and impulsivity as exceptions or "imperfections" of reason. The judiciary recognises a psychological duality to humans but only ever to the psychologically ill, thus assuming the healthy as capable of full rationality.

3.3 The Duality of Reason and Emotion

In neuroscience, legal theoretical frameworks can find scientific grounding in the dualistic dynamic between emotion and cognition. The belief that men are inherently rational beings underlined much of human history – representing the theoretical background that, although challenged theoretically, has continued to ground the legal system. Reason and emotion have long been conceived as separate and opposing forces, with emotion representing the animalistic and instinctive side of men being controlled and overpowered by deliberate and logical thinking.[11] This dualistic dynamic, however, evolved through the years and has been embodied in theories of emotion that have progressively recognised it as a more eminent function. For example, Damasio's "Somatic Marker" theory granted that emotions, via physiological responses, may guide decision-making and rationality.[12] Similarly, scientific details have emerged and highlighted areas of the brain that represent an interface between cognition and emotion (e.g., the ventromedial prefrontal cortex) that can affect decision-making.[13]

For the last several decades, emotions have been extensively demonstrated to impact different aspects of cognition, such as perception, attention, and decision-making;[14] it has become clear that the conception of emotion and cognition as separate phenomena has been misleading. Cognition and emotion constantly and bidirectionally interact, forming a vicious cycle of reciprocal activation. For example, integral emotions (i.e., emotions arising from a judgement or choice) might benefit choices by emotionally or somatically marking the options but could occasionally constitute a strong bias.[15] A famous example of integral emotions' bias is that of people who fear flying but who might choose to drive

11 T. Brosch, 'The Impact of Emotion on Perception, Attention, Memory, and Decision-Making' [2013] *Swiss Medical Weekly* 1–2.
12 A. Bechara, 'Emotion, Decision Making and the Orbitofrontal Cortex' (2000) 10 *Cerebral Cortex* 295.
13 J. S. Lerner et al., 'Emotion and Decision Making' (2015) 66 *Annual Review of Psychology* 799.
14 Supra note. 9.
15 Supra note. 11.

instead – thus making a disadvantageous choice regardless of the presence of cognitive information suggesting otherwise.[16]

A more subtle and interesting effect on decision-making comes from emotions carried over from a different choice or experience.[17] Several studies have found that emotional states or moods from previous situations can influence choice by affecting appraisals of situations and by determining the content and depth of thought behind decisions.[18] Indeed, each emotion serves a specific coordination and motivational function, and it thus carries its action tendency, implicit goals and appraisal themes; even emotions of the same valence, such as anger and sadness, have indeed been found to differ in several ways, resulting in significantly different effects on decision-making.[19] For example, a negative mood, in general, has been found to lead to more pessimistic assessments of situations and increased risk perception.[20]

Analysis based on appraisal theories has highlighted how each emotion predisposes us to interpret and understand a situation in a particular manner according to functional goals. For instance, anger and pride are amply characterised by the appraisal of events as caused by individuals, either the self or others (increasing perceived responsibility) and are highly predictable. On the contrary, sadness and surprise are characterised by the appraisal of circumstantial or situational control (alleviating the perceived responsibility of the individual). The perceived unpredictability of the situation characterises them.[21] These appraisal themes suggest that emotional states, such as anger and pride, will produce a high level of perceived control and responsibility in situations, reflecting on the assessment of data used for decision-making; the same goes for emotions such as sadness and surprise, which can produce a low level of perceived individual responsibility.

Other effects of specific emotional states are related to the depth of information processing each emotion might produce because of its functional purpose. For example, fear is an affective state that signals a threat,

---

16 G. Loewenstein, 'Out of Control: Visceral Influences on Behavior' (1996) 65 *Organizational Behavior and Human Decision Processes* 272.

17 S. Han, J. S Lerner, D. Keltner, 'Feelings and Consumer Decision Making: The Appraisal-Tendency Framework' (2007) 17 *Journal of Consumer Psychology* 158; D. Keltner, J. S Lerner, "Emotion" *Handbook of Social Psychology* (New York, Wiley, 2010) 317–352.

18 J. S. Lerner et al., (2015) 799.

19 R. Adolphs, D. J Anderson, *The Neuroscience of Emotion: A New Synthesis* (Princeton University Press, New Jersey, 2018) 65, 85.

20 E. J. Johnson, A. Tversky, 'Affect, Generalization, and the Perception of Risk.' (1983) 45 *Journal of Personality and Social Psychology* 20.

21 D. Keltner, P. C. Ellsworth, K. Edwards, 'Beyond Simple Pessimism: Effects of Sadness and Anger on Social Perception.' (1993) 64 *Journal of Personality and Social Psychology* 740.

thus producing a high level of vigilance and information processing.[22] A few studies particularly show that positive affective states, as opposed to negative, tend to lead to higher reliance on heuristic cues and stereotypes.[23] Other studies suggested that the level of certainty characterising each emotional state determines the level of a person's reliance on heuristics, stereotypes and attention to detail; high-certainty emotions, such as pride, anger and happiness, tend to result in higher reliance on stereotypes, heuristics, and lower attention to the details of an argument, as opposed to low certainty emotions such as sadness and fear, which show the opposed pattern.[24]

The legal context has continued to be based on the old conceptions of human behaviour, relying on the notion of human rationality prevailing on emotions. Indeed, changes to conceptions of the duality of reason and emotion and, more particularly, knowledge of emotion's effects on decisional processes are only starting to have a more substantial role in legal decision-making. Indeed, knowledge of the function of the orbitofrontal cortex as a regulator of impulse, for example, has allowed its dysfunctions to become a legal defence.[25] The system is starting to accept that dynamics between emotion and cognition are complex and might be compromised.

However, the understanding that rational decision-making is strongly influenced by forces other than reason has yet to impact legal frameworks concretely. The implications for these effects appear clear; if a legal choice involving all effects of human decisional processes can be governed by external influences such as incidental emotions, it cannot be entirely based on rules (e.g., laws). Indeed, emotions can constitute biases and direct choices according to their effects on cognition. Imagine, for example, a judge with a personal prejudice towards a defence lawyer; his presence in a case might provoke an unconscious angry reaction and thus bias a judge's decisional processes in a way that might be disadvantageous and even unfair for the defendant. Indeed, anger may encourage the

---

22 N. Schwarz, 'Feelings as Information: Informational and Motivational Functions of Affective States' in E. T. R. Higgins, E. T, R. M. Sorrentino (eds), *Handbook of Motivation and Cognition*, Volume 2 (Guildford Press, 1st Edition, New York,1990) pp. 527–561.

23 H. Bless et al., 'Mood and the Use of Scripts: Does a Happy Mood Really Lead to Mindlessness?' (1996) 71 *Journal of Personality and Social Psychology* 665.

24 L. Z. Tiedens, S. Linton, 'Judgment under Emotional Certainty and Uncertainty: The Effects of Specific Emotions on Information Processing' (2001) 81 *Journal of Personality and Social Psychology* 973.

25 F. Coppola, 'We are More Than our Executive Functions: on the Emotional and Situational Aspects of Criminal Responsibility and Punishment' 16(2) *Criminal Law and Philosophy* 1–14.

perception of responsibility, which could likely enhance perceived legal culpability in such a context.

3.4 Empathy and Decision-Making

We have established that emotion can inform decision-making by affecting attention, perception, and appraisal. In the context of social decision-making, we experience our own feelings and are continuously exposed to other people's expressions of feelings, which can affect us differently. Exposure to another's affective state has been proven to have the potential to provoke similar emotions in the observer; this phenomenon is referred to as emotional contagion. This emotional transmission happens unconsciously through a vicarious neural response – likely using mirror neurons, which respond both to the performance of an action and the observation of the same action being performed. Recently, these neurons have been found in brain areas associated with emotion, such as the anterior insula and the cingulate cortex, when experiencing and observing others' emotional states in instances of disgust and fear.[26]

In other cases, interpersonal emotions can affect decision-making as a function of the complementary emotion they evoke in the decision-maker.[27] For example, in the cases of anger[28] and gratitude,[29] such emotions seem to trigger concessions from others. The extent to which we can observe these effects in a specific context, however, highly depends on the ability of the interacting parties to display emotions and process emotional information. Emotionally intelligent individuals are supposedly better at understanding others' states and eliciting the desired emotions in others, thus affecting the outcomes of others' decisions and behaviours.[30] Let us think now of a courtroom in which a defendant, but also his lawyer and anyone else in the room, might be expressing fear, anger, sadness or any other emotion; this has the potential to affect a judge or other decision-maker by eliciting an emotional response in him, which in turn might regulate his behaviour – creating an ulterior source of variability in decision-making for which it is hard to account.

26 *The Empathic Brain* (YouTube 2018) (accessed 2022) <https://www.youtube.com/watch?v=Yw8p2D2Jejg> (accessed 2022).
27 J. S. Lerner et al., (2015) 799.
28 G. A. Van Kleef, C. K. De Dreu, A. S. Manstead, 'The Interpersonal Effects of Anger and Happiness in Negotiations.' (2004) 86 *Journal of Personality and Social Psychology* 57.
29 B. Rind, P. Bordia, 'Effect of Server's 'Thank You' and Personalization on Restaurant Tipping' (1995) 25 *Journal of Applied Social Psychology* 745.
30 G. A. Van Kleef, C. K. De Dreu, A. S. Manstead, 'The Interpersonal Effects of Emotions in Negotiations: A Motivated Information Processing Approach.' (2004) 87 *Journal of Personality and Social Psychology* 510.

Another way in which the emotional state of others can affect a decision-maker is through empathy – defined as a combined phenomenon constituting both a visceral, bodily response (referred to as experience sharing) and a cognitive response (referred to as mentalising); both components of empathic responses have been commonly described as automatic and instinctive reactions in healthy individuals.[31] Recent literature on empathy, however, is beginning to highlight a new property of empathic responses: their motivational nature. Thus, such work begins to recognise the importance of context in the perception, understanding, and experience of other's internal states.

This is particularly important if we consider empathy as a precursor of prosocial behaviour, such as voluntary actions intended to benefit or help others. Differences in the amplitude of empathic responses are intuitively present in the population; indeed, the extent to which an individual reflects on other's motivations and the accuracy to which an individual pinpoints the mental state of others show high variability, with an extreme example being people affected by autism who are notably impaired in their mentalising capacities.[32] The origins of differences in the tendency to understand and resonate with other's internal states have often been attributed to differences in neural structures and personality – defining empathy as a trait that can vary across individuals but remains relatively stable across different situations.[33] Recent reports, however, deeply question these assumptions.

The conception of empathy as a motivated phenomenon may account for the role that individual cognitive assumptions, as well as individual goals and other contextual factors, have in determining whether an observer has an empathic response. In particular, Zaki[34] identified six contextual factors regulating one's propensity to respond empathically. Among these, interference with competition and affiliation is the most interesting. Interference with competition refers to the un-favorableness of feeling empathy towards someone who belongs to a different social group. Indeed, at an evolutionary level, engaging in empathic responses with members of other social groups could impair competition by eliciting pro-sociality and compromising the determination to "win" a needed resource. The desire for affiliation is the approaching counterpart of this motive; it refers to the recognised value of coalition between group

31 J. Zaki, 'Empathy: A Motivated Account.' (2014) 140 *Psychological Bulletin* 1608.
32 F. Castelli, 'Mind, Theories of' in J. D. Wright, (eds) *International Encyclopedia of the Social and Behavioral Sciences* 2nd edition, Vol.15 (Elsevier, 2nd Edition, Oxford) pp. 539–544.
33 Supra note. 33.
34 Ibid.

members, which encourages empathy between members even when personally and materially costly for the individual since it promotes future cooperation. It emerges that the likeliness to engage in an empathic response is amply determined by a complex computation of motivational pros and cons, which are individually and situationally tailored – but that generally tend to favour those who belong to our own "group" and greatly disadvantage those whom we consider as being different from us.[35]

Motives also regulate empathic responses through regulatory strategies, which often precede vicarious neural responses and inferences on others' intentions and occur outside our awareness.[36] We can, thus, understand our beliefs, biases and stereotypes as gatekeepers for empathy, regulating our response from the backstage of our awareness. One of the main forms of appraisals to regulate empathic responses is mentally asserting that a person experiencing negative affect deserves it or is uniquely responsible for it – diminishing empathic responses. Let us remember what we previously stated on the effects of high-certainty emotions on decision-making. We pointed to anger, particularly as increasing the perception of human responsibility and diminishing that of situational influences. It appears clear now that not only previous beliefs on individuals' group belongings can affect the extent to which we engage in empathy, but the emotions we are feeling – as incidental, integral or vicariously perceived – have a determining role in tipping the balance in decision-making.

3.5 Empathy, Decision-Making, and Vulnerable Defendants

This renewed conception of empathy, as a force that, in its nature, is biased and biases behaviour, challenges our understanding of decisions within legal systems. Decisional processes appear to be controlled not solely by data, laws, and reason but by our and others' emotions, beliefs, and biases. This results in a computation so complex that, although we might be taught to have a sense of awareness about our emotional states that can help define the boundaries of their influence, our minds remain, for the most part, actual computational "black boxes" that produce outcomes from inputs through untraceable rules and biases.

This becomes especially problematic in cases of vulnerable defendants. While judges and lawyers have remained quite steadfast in their beliefs that objective rationality and motivational transparency are possible in legal decision-making, one can imagine that emotional aspects of cases

---

35 Ibid.
36 Ibid.

involving vulnerable defendants are likely stronger than in many other cases; indeed, although research is lacking on this matter, we can well imagine that beliefs and emotions about particularly defined and generally marginalised groups are stronger, be it in positive or negative terms, compared to those on random members of society.

Specific forms of vulnerability appear to be especially interesting, such as defendants with antisocial personality disorder and autism spectrum disorder. Some characterising symptomatology of these disorders include general disturbances of social and emotional behaviour.[37] We have stressed the effects that others' emotions can have on observers – either by unconsciously eliciting an affective state in others through emotional contagion, experience sharing, or by informing mentalising processes. People with autism spectrum disorder have difficulties displaying emotion and with social understanding; these differences can influence how they communicate, express emotions, and show intentions to such an extent that their internal states can be entirely misunderstood.[38] Conversely, those affected by antisocial personality disorder may be able to "turn on and off" their empathy and social skills; these individuals might encourage positive responses by overplaying their emotions and lying about their intentions and beliefs to provoke an empathic response in others purposely.[39]

There is great variability across individual decision-makers and situations regarding cognitive biases and neural noise. The same defendant can be judged in contrasting ways simply based on the personal experiences of the decision-maker and his propensity, ability, or willingness to engage in an empathic response. In the same way, different defendants accused of the same crime can be judged drastically differently by the same individual due to the defendant's social-group belonging or his ability to display emotion. In the cases of vulnerable defendants, defendants with autism might have difficulties displaying emotion, while those with an antisocial personality disorder may be particularly skilled at turning emotions on and off as needed. The consequences of this become situational judgements of justice, a level of unpredictability in legal outcomes, and a hinted attack on our conception of ideal legal reasoning,

---

37 American Psychiatric Association, *Diagnostic and statistical Manual of Mental Disorders* (American Psychiatric Association, 5th Edition, Text Review) 31. (Accessed April 2023) <https://dsm.psychiatryonline.org/doi/book/10.1176/appi.books.9780890425787>.

38 C. Keysers, H. Meffert, V. Gazzola, 'Reply: Spontaneous versus Deliberate Vicarious Representations: Different Routes to Empathy in Psychopathy and Autism' (2014) vol.137 (4) *Brain: A Journal of Neurology* 273.

39 Supra note. 40.

Thus, this ultimately presents us with a controversial situation in which we understand that legal choices are not entirely "rational" and not minimally transparent – where factors such as what somebody has eaten for breakfast can have an immeasurable impact on legal outcomes and, more so, the identity of an individual outside of his crime and his ability to evoke empathy can determine the outcome of the legal choice. This particularly poses great discrimination issues for defendants belonging to minority social groups. Indeed, we are confronted with the controversial and scientifically grounded understanding that humans are "black boxes" to their personal and subjective judgment.

3.6 Conclusions and Artificial Intelligence

The advancement of technological systems, such as those of AI, has represented a possible alternative to the inescapable subjectivity and noisiness that defines human choices[40]. Neuroscientific findings laid the grounds for theoretical frameworks, such as legal realism, that have a concrete impact on the understanding of law and justice. We have highlighted how accounts of emotional experiences and processes may blur the lines between reason (cognition) and emotion and how research on empathic responses can show its biases and biasing nature. This work describes the human decisional process as effectively opaque in contexts involving others and ourselves.

It is natural to ask whether human legal decisions can be considered legally transparent or relied upon for justice. The advent of AI raises – in the face of the issues stemming from the human decisional process that we have discussed here – concerns regarding whether AI can combat these issues and whether a rule-based system is truly desirable within a socially relevant framework. Indubitably, AI represents a much more reliable and objective classification system, considering it is hardly capable of responding to emotional triggers or people's affective states. Indeed, although both algorithmic and data biases are often pinpointed as a pitfall of technology, it is seldom considered that, contrary to human biases, technological biases are much easier to detect and correct. We are thus induced to reflect on which integral or circumstantial aspects we believe should weigh on legal decisions. Do we consider empathy, emotional contagion and emotional states as biases to be avoided or, instead, as essential aspects of social decisions and human morality? What role can AI play in legal decisions, considering its independence from

---

40 D.Kahneman, O. R. Sibony, C. R. Sunstein, *Noise, A flaw in Human Judgment*, (Little, Brown and Company 2021) 165.

empathy and emotion? Can our understanding of machine-made decisions change considering the understanding that humans themselves are "black boxes"?

Prakken and Sartor point out that law is not just a conceptual and axiomatic system but has social objectives and effects, and it may be called upon and applied in circumstances not foreseen at the time of its approval; the authors conclude that the orientation of law to the future and unforeseen situations often means the law will far transcend the definition of rule-based decisions.[41] AI, in this sense, might fail to grasp all that goes beyond the literal and result in reducing law and justice to empty formulas.

Moreover, in theoretical terms, the question of the nature and interpretation of the results of algorithms is at the forefront. Following Kevin Ashley's detailed analysis, we can stress that

> "since a Machine Learning (ML) algorithm learns rules based on statistical regularities that may surprise humans, its rules may not necessarily seem reasonable to humans. ML predictions are data-driven. Sometimes the data contain features that, for spurious reasons such as coincidence or biased selection, happen to be associated with the outcomes of cases in a particular collection. Although machine-induced rules may lead to accurate predictions, they do not refer to human expertise and may not be as intelligible to humans as an expert's manually constructed rules. Since the rules the ML algorithm infers do not necessarily reflect explicit legal knowledge or expertise, they may not correspond to a human expert's criteria of reasonableness."[42]

Clearly, complex forms of AI pose important challenges regarding legal justification and motivation; indeed, artificial, machine-made rules might not be retraceable to clearly existing laws and legislations and are consequently hardly contestable by opposing parties.

The automatisation of legal decisional processes also affects processes of legal argumentation, and, according to some authors, can deprive lawyers and judges of their full independence and autonomy of argument.[43] Indeed, the main issue that AI in law seems to introduce is a lack of

41 H. Prakken, G. Sartor, 'Law and Logic: A Review from an Argumentation Perspective' (2015) 227 *Artificial Intelligence* 214.

42 K. D. Ashley, *Artificial Intelligence and Legal Analytics: New Tools for Law Practice in the Digital Age* (Cambridge University Press, Cambridge, 2017) 111.

43 A. Giordano, 'Intelligenza Artificiale e Giusto Processo Civile,' *L'intelligenza artificiale tra scienza, etica e diritto* (Munera 2022) 120.

general flexibility of outcome; although able to modify their own rules, in fact, ML mechanisms are hardly able to accommodate arguments, failing to go beyond the literal meanings of legal norms and pattern-derived rules. This poses the question of how to combine the intrinsic nature of patterns emerging from legal analytics (and their limited explainability) and the right to an explanation of public (and sometimes even private) legal decisions.

AI thus highlights the importance of the "human" within social justice and law frameworks – stressing the importance of flexibility and independence as essential values within the law and recognising that law is not an axiomatic system that can be reduced to a mathematical formula. Yet, simultaneously, it points to the pitfalls of human reasoning and decisions. It should be noted that the relationship between law and decision-making, and between law and AI, is intertwined with legal traditions, scientific knowledge, and the orientations present in the AI debate. This gives rise to complex practical, theoretical, and moral questions that are yet to be answered and that we by no means attempt to answer in this piece. Can a combination of different legal approaches, accommodating AI and human decisional processes, be used? Can the obligation to motivate be fulfilled if machine learning is used or if it is not used? Could AI also organise activities that do not appear explicable in rational terms?

In conclusion, AI–neuroscience–law entanglement may closely resemble an intricate intersection of different and branching paths which need further exploration. We must begin to disentangle them, particularly for vulnerable defendants, to make for a better functioning, and perhaps a more objective and reliable, legal system.

4 Safeguarding the Procedural Rights of Young Defendants in England and Wales

The Role of Neuroscience

Amy Sixsmith

4.1 Introduction

The European Convention on Human Rights guarantees all defendants the right to a fair trial. In *Stanford v UK* [1994], the European Court of Human Rights confirmed that this right encompasses "the right of an accused to participate effectively in a criminal trial."[1] This right to effective participation is "implicit in the very notion of an adversarial procedure"[2] and is an intrinsic element of procedural justice. However, despite the importance of a defendant's participatory rights, the precise scope of the right to effective participation remains unclear.[3] Cases, such as *SC v United Kingdom*,[4] have attempted to outline the core competencies required for effective participation, however, case law does not stipulate how a defendant's ability to participate effectively can be determined, monitored, or attained.[5] As a result, concerns have been raised about the extent to which the law in England and Wales safeguards the right to effective participation, particularly in the cases of young defendants.[6] This is despite the fact that the law makes provision for special measures and modifications to be utilised to facilitate a young defendant's effective participation in proceedings.

This chapter argues that the legal framework for assessing and evaluating young defendants' effective participation is inadequate and this may render the participation of many young defendants "non-participatory" or "tokenistic", undermining their right to effective participation guaranteed by Article 6 of the ECHR. Furthermore, it uses neuroscientific

---

1 *Stanford v UK* [1994] ECHR 6, at [26].
2 n1.
3 A. Owusu-Bempah. 'The Interpretation and Application of the Right to Effective Participation' (2018) 22(4) *International Journal of Evidence & Proof* 321, 323.
4 *SC v United Kingdom* (2005) 40 EHRR 10.
5 n3.
6 n3.

DOI: 10.4324/9781003331056-5

research to argue that young defendants are, by virtue of their age and corresponding biological immaturity, prone to experience participatory difficulties and that such research highlights the need for a more effective legal framework to secure young defendants' rights to effective participation. It argues that neuroscientific research could, and should, be used to inform future policy developments.

4.2 The Right to Participate Effectively in Criminal Trials

To provide context to the thesis of this chapter, it is first necessary to summarise how the current legal framework for assessing and evaluating the extent to which young defendants can participate in a trial has developed. In the context of criminal law, the right to effective participation is an intrinsic element of procedural justice that ensures that those accused of criminal offences can participate meaningfully in proceedings instituted against them. A criminal trial is a process through which a defendant's criminal liability is formally determined and is concerned with whether or not a defendant satisfies the conditions of criminal liability.[7] If the prosecution is able to prove that the conditions of criminal liability are satisfied, the defendant is convicted of the offence(s) specified in the indictment. If the conditions of criminal liability are not proven, the defendant is acquitted.[8] However, as Duff has observed, there are also "preconditions" of criminal liability "which must be met if the trial is to be possible, or legitimate, at all."[9]

An important precondition of criminal liability relates to a defendant's capacity to be tried. As Duff has observed, the purpose of a trial is to call the defendant to answer the charge against him so he must be able to understand the charge and respond to it. "If he cannot understand it, or the process by which it is adjudicated, he cannot answer it; his trial, if it went ahead, would be a travesty."[10] If a trial is to be legitimate and fair, a defendant must be capable of being an active participant in their trial and must be able to engage in proceedings in a meaningful way. In England and Wales, a defendant's participatory rights are protected by Article 6 of the ECHR.

The right to effective participation under Article 6(3) helps to "ensure that the defendant is treated as the autonomous subject of the

---

7 A. R. Duff., 'Law, Language and Community: Some Preconditions of Criminal Liability' (1998) 2 *Oxford Journal of Legal Studies* 189, 193.

8 n7, 193.

9 n7, 193.

10 n7, 194.

proceedings, and not simply as an object for the imposition of conviction and punishment" because "a defendant cannot have a fair trial if they cannot participate effectively."[11] The right to effective participation also extends to young defendants, which has been confirmed in cases such as *SC v United Kingdom*[12] and *T and V v United Kingdom*.[13]

The trial of a young defendant does in itself constitute a breach of Article 6. This was confirmed in the case of *T and V v United Kingdom*,[14] which concerned the trial of two young boys convicted of murdering a toddler in 1993. The case attracted widespread media attention not only because of the brutal nature of the murder but because the accused were both just ten years old when the offence was committed.[15] The ECtHR judgment recognised that children are prone to experience participatory issues and stressed that "it is essential that a child charged with an offence is dealt with in a manner which takes full account of his age, level of maturity and intellectual and emotional capacities, and that steps are taken to promote his ability to understand and participate in the proceedings."[16] It is therefore essential that, where necessary, steps are taken to facilitate the effective participation of young defendants. A failure to implement measures that enable a young defendant to participate in proceedings effectively may amount to a breach of the right to a fair trial, as illustrated in the case of *V and T*.

The ECtHR held that the trial of the defendants (V and T), which took place in the Crown Court, constituted a breach of Article 6 because the defendants could not effectively participate in proceedings. This was so even though modifications had been made to take account of their young age, such as shortened hearing times, regular breaks, seating the applicants next to social workers and near to their lawyers and parents, and using a raised dock so that the defendants could see the proceedings. However, insufficient accommodations were put in place to account for the defendants' level of understanding and maturity; the judge and counsel wore wigs and gowns, and because of significant public and media interest in the case, the courtroom, press benches and public gallery were full. This lead the trial judge, in his summation, to acknowledge that the public interest in the case had been distressing for the defendants and asked the jury to consider this notion when evaluating the evidence. Most significantly, the trial conditions and the defendants' disturbed emotional

---

11 n3, 323.
12 n4.
13 *T and V v United Kingdom* (2000) *30 EHRR 121*.
14 *n16* at para [86].
15 G. Rice and T. Thomas, 'James Bulger - A Matter of Public Interest' (2013) 21 *International Journal of Child Rights* 1.
16 *n16*.

states were deemed to have prevented the defendants from participating effectively in their proceedings. Therefore, in response to the judgment, Practice Direction (2010)[17] was issued, stating that the normal trial process should be adapted to assist young defendants in understanding and participating in proceedings. This Consolidated Criminal Practice Direction applies to the trial of young people in the Crown Court.

In cases where a defendant cannot effectively participate, the proceedings should be stayed as an abuse of process, as it is not possible for the defendant to have a fair trial.[18] However, it is important to note that staying proceedings as an abuse of process remains a discretionary remedy rarely exercised, particularly in the youth court;[19] it can be used only in "exceptional circumstances."[20] The only alternative is that a defendant who is unable to effectively participate in proceedings may be deemed "unfit to plead."[21] However, this is also problematic as this process can only apply to a trial on indictment and would therefore apply only to a young defendant on trial in the Crown Court.

The common law test for unfitness to plead, established in the case of *R v Pritchard*, applies to courts of summary jurisdiction.[22] The threshold for establishing that a defendant is unfit to plead is difficult to satisfy, and it is unlikely that a young defendant facing participatory issues would be deemed unfit to plead without evidence of severe impairment.[23] Indeed, the precise relationship between the concepts of effective participation and unfitness to plead is ambiguous and is in urgent need of clarification.[24] Although young defendants enjoy the right to effective participation, there is currently no coherent process through which a young defendant's ability to participate effectively can be evaluated and addressed. Further, there is a risk that young defendants facing participatory difficulties may not be diverted from criminal proceedings through unfitness to plead or through a stay of proceedings, thereby undermining their rights under Article 6.

---

17 Consolidated Criminal Practice Direction 2007.

18 n3, 329.

19 R. Arthur, 'Giving Effect to Young People's Right to Participate Effectively in Criminal Proceedings' (2016) 28(3) *Child and Family Law Quarterly* 223, 236.

20 *R (Ebrahim) v Feltham Magistrates' Court* [2001] EWHC Admin 130, [2001] 1 WLR 1293, at para [17]; *Attorney General's Reference* (No 1 of 1990) [1992] QB 630, at [643].

21 Criminal Procedure (Insanity) Act 1964, as amended by the Criminal Procedure (Insanity and Unfitness to Plead) Act 1991 and the Domestic Violence, Crime and Victims Act 2004.

22 *R v Pritchard* (1836) 7 C & P 303.

23 n19, 225.

24 Law Commission, *Unfitness to Plead Volume 1: Report* Number 364 (HMSO, London, 2016), para 1.43. See also n3, 323.

The Law Commission has stated that the lack of a coherent procedure through which a person's unfitness to plead or capacity for effective participation is the "most fundamental deficiency of the current summary system."[25] The Commission's view was that the test for unfitness to plead is inadequate, particularly with regard to young defendants. It, therefore, recommended that the test be reformulated "as an assessment of the defendant's capacity to participate effectively in a trial."[26] The Commission felt that such a reformulation would address the lack of alignment between the unfitness to plead test and the separate test of effective participation, as set out in *SC*.[27] Importantly, the Commission believed "effective participation should be prioritised as the concept most likely to capture the meaningful engagement with which fitness to plead is centrally concerned."[28] Thus, the Commission argued that reframing the test in the way that they proposed would better recognise and safeguard the right to effective participation. However, before this can be properly analysed, the parameters of what is meant by "participate effectively" need to be established. Therefore, the next section of this chapter provides a critical discussion of the requirements for effective participation.

4.3 Requirements for Effective Participation

It is problematic for these purposes that the legal concept of effective participation is not statutorily defined.[29] However, the requirements of effective participation have been outlined through case law. The leading authority here is the case of *SC*, which concerned the trial of a young boy, and established that effective participation:

> presupposes that the accused has a broad understanding of the nature of the trial process and of what is at stake for him or her, including the significance of any penalty which may be imposed. It means that he or she, if necessary with the assistance of, for example, an interpreter, lawyer, social worker or friend, should be able to understand the general thrust of what is said in court. The defendant should be able to follow what is said by the prosecution witnesses and, if represented, to explain to his own lawyers his version of events, point out

25 n24, para 7.13.
26 n24.
27 n24.
28 n24.
29 G. McKeever et al 'The Snakes and Ladders of Legal Participation: Litigants in Person and the Right to a Fair Trial under Article 6 of the European Convention on Human Rights' (2022) 49(1) *Journal of Law and Society* 1, 7.

any statements with which he disagrees and make them aware of any facts which should be put forward in his defence.[30]

As Owusu-Bempah has explained, this is the most comprehensive statement of effective participation provided by the courts. "It implies that, overall, defendants should be able to maintain a level of general understanding and active engagement throughout the trial."[31] The *SC* formulation was extended further in the case *R v John M*, so the test now includes the defendant's ability to give evidence in his own defence. [32] The test for effective participation requires that the defendant understands the case against them, follow the course of proceedings, instruct their legal representative(s), and give evidence in their defence. Thus, evaluating what each component requires before considering neuroscientific research about young defendants' capacity to fulfil these requirements is important.

Firstly, the judge in the case of *SC* outlined that a defendant understands the case before them. This means that the defendant must have "a broad understanding of the nature of the trial process, and of what is at stake for him or her including the significance of any penalty which may be imposed."[33] It is important to note that the defendant need not understand the finer points of law or procedure or follow every aspect of proceedings, but they do need to understand the general nature of proceedings and comprehend the significance of their decisions made during the trial. The defendant should also be able to grasp the role of critical legal actors and understand the consequences of being convicted.

Secondly, the defendant must be able to follow the course of the trial proceedings. This requires the defendant to "understand the general thrust of what is said in court" and "follow what is said by the prosecution witnesses."[34] This is because the Law Commission has stated,

> the purpose of the defendant being able to follow what occurs in court is to facilitate an understanding of the case, so that he or she can advance an alternative account or instruct a representative to do so on his or her behalf.[35]

---

30 n4 [29].
31 n3, 325.
32 *R v John M* [2003] EWCA Crim 3452.
33 n4 at [29].
34 n4 at [29].
35 n24, para 3.102.

This requires the defendant to have the capacity to concentrate on proceedings and comprehend what is being said by various legal actors. The Law Commission believed this ability was "critical to the ability to play an active part in the proceedings."[36]

Thirdly, the defendant must have the capacity to instruct solicitors and counsel. This requires a defendant to be able to convey intelligibly to their lawyers what they wish them to advance and put forward in their defence. In *John M*, the court stated that this requires the defendant to be able to understand the questions posed by their lawyers, use his or her mind to answer them, and convey intelligibly the answers they wish to give.[37] In *SC*, the court confirmed that a defendant must possess the ability "to explain to his own lawyers his version of events, point out any statements with which he disagrees, and make them aware of any facts which should be put forward in his defence."[38]

Finally, the defendant must be able to give evidence in their own defence. This requires the person to understand the questions asked and communicate responses to questions, including the ability to recount events intelligibly and coherently.

The current test, therefore, provides a useful starting point for assessing a defendant's capacity for effective participation. However, much of the wording suggests that participation is a straightforward binary question; it does not accommodate the nuances involved in determining whether a young defendant can effectively participate in proceedings. Research has demonstrated that effective participation requires much more than passive participation in legal proceedings. As McKeever has pointed out, "participation in legal hearings is not a binary process," whereby a defendant either participates or does not participate.[39] There are "different types of legal participation, defined by the extent to which the intellectual, practical, emotional and attitudinal barriers to participation can be managed or overcome."[40] McKeever has further argued that in legal contexts where participatory barriers are not managed or overcome, a person's participation in legal proceedings may be categorised as "tokenistic" or "non-participatory."[41] In reflecting on McKeever's analysis, a young person's participation in criminal proceedings should only

---

36 n24, para 3.91.
37 n32 at [24].
38 *SC v United Kingdom* (2005) 40 EHRR 10 (App No 60958/00) at [29].
39 G. McKeever, 'Remote Justice? Litigants in Person and Participation in Court Processes during COVID-19' (2020) 005 *MLR Forum* (available from: http://www.modernlawreview.co.uk/mckeever-remote-justice) 4.
40 G. McKeever, 'A Ladder of Legal Participation for Tribunal Users' (2013) 3 *Public Law* 573.
41 n39.

be regarded as effective when participatory barriers have been identified and appropriately addressed through special measures and modifications. This analysis is consistent with the judgment in *V and T*, as discussed above, which illustrated that adjustments and modifications for young defendants must be sufficient to enable the defendant's effective participation. It is, therefore, essential that procedural safeguards are in place to ensure that participatory barriers are identified and, where possible, are addressed by implementing special measures and modifications. Such a system is necessary to ensure that young defendants can achieve the standard required for effective participation in a criminal trial in England and Wales.

There has, however, been some movement towards reform. The Law Commission has recommended that the test be reformulated and set out in statute and that it should consider the following abilities:

a) an ability to understand the nature of the charge;

b) an ability to understand the evidence adduced as evidence of the commission of the offence;

c) an ability to understand the trial process and the consequences of being convicted;

d) an ability to give instructions to a legal representative;

e) an ability to make a decision about whether to plead guilty or not guilty;

f) an ability to make a decision about whether to give evidence;

g) an ability to make other decisions that might need to be made by the defendant in connection with the trial;

h) an ability to follow the proceedings in court on the offence;

i) an ability to give evidence;

j) any other ability that appears to the court to be relevant in the particular case.[42]

The proposed test is largely comprised of components of the effective participation test laid out in *SC*; however, it also encompasses the ability to give evidence and any other ability that appears to the court to be relevant in a particular case. If adopted, the Commission's proposal would result

---

42 n24, clause 3(4).

in a more flexible and wide-ranging framework than the current test for effective participation.

The overarching contention of this chapter is that the legal framework for assessing and evaluating young defendants' effective participation is inadequate and may render the participation of many young defendants "non-participatory" or "tokenistic", undermining their right to effective participation guaranteed by Article 6 of the ECHR. It has so far set out what the existing test is, identified where that test may run into difficulty with its lack of flexibility and failure to take into adequate consideration the varying grades of participation a young defendant can achieve before their participation is properly regarded as being fully effective and discussed the current proposals for reform. This is therefore an appropriate juncture to introduce the second element of this chapter's thesis, which is advocating for the involvement of neuroscience. The following section illustrates how neuroscientific research may be able to provide valuable insights into how maturation processes, which occur throughout childhood and adolescence, can impact young defendants' ability to participate effectively in criminal proceedings. This research demonstrates that young defendants are prone to experience participatory difficulties and suggests they will likely require additional assistance to achieve effective participation at trial.

4.4 Neuroscientific Research and the Ability to Participate Effectively in Criminal Proceedings

Although "[o]ne need not be a scientist to know that young humans differ from older ones,"[43] our understanding of why and how children and young people differ from adults is continuously developing. Neuroscientific research has enabled us to better understand how the human brain develops over childhood and adolescence and is helping us understand the developmental processes that might affect children and young people's abilities to exercise cognitive and socio-emotional capacities.[44] For example, research conducted using brain imaging techniques demonstrates that the behaviour of children and young people is, at the very least, influenced by brain development and function.[45] Such research is also thought to help to explain why young people exhibit particular behavioural traits. How the brain develops and functions during ado-

---

43 O. Jones, J. D. Schall, F. X.Shen *Law and neuroscience* (2 edn, Aspen Publishing, 2020) 694.

44 E. Cauffman, L. Steinberg 'Emerging Findings from Research on Adolescent Development and Juvenile Justice' (2012) 7 *Victims and Offenders* 428, 432.

45 n43, 697–705.

lescence is considered to increase adolescents' likelihood of risk-taking behaviour and increase their susceptibility to peer pressure.[46] This is thought to be attributable to the fact that "the frontal brain regions, which are related to organisation, planning, and inhibitory control, are not fully developed until the end of adolescence" whereas "regions that are reward-sensitive and regions connected to emotions are generally more active during adolescence."[47] Brain imaging findings support this view, which strongly suggests that adolescents exhibit such behaviour because of the brain's biological immaturity.[48]

These findings have led some scholars to argue that this should render adolescents less culpable for their behaviour. In contrast, others have argued that such claims overstate the significance of neuroscientific research findings.[49] However, this chapter concerns potentially less contentious aspects of neuroscientific research: how brain development during childhood and adolescence impacts a young person's ability to participate in criminal proceedings effectively. The human brain matures throughout childhood and adolescence. The World Health Organization states that adolescence begins at the age of 10 and lasts until the age of 19.[50] The physical changes that occur during this period are substantial; consequently, there are significant structural and functional differences between the brains of adults and young people.[51] Because of this, children and young people are considered "developmentally immature" compared to adults. In this context, developmental immaturity refers to "normative but incomplete development amongst youths, as compared with adults."[52] There is significant individual variability of brain development during this period, as development occurs at different rates and speeds. This means that although older adolescents are generally more developed than their younger counterparts, some will be developmentally immature compared to peers within their age group because each person develops according to their own individual pathway.[53] While generalisations can mask significant heterogeneity in the timing of neuromaturation,[54] research provides

46 K. Haines et al 'Children and Crime: In the Moment' (2021) 21(3) *Youth Justice* 275, 281. See also E. Mercurio et al 'Adolescent Brain Development and Progressive Legal Responsibility in the Latin American Context' (2020) 11 *Frontiers in Psychology* 627.
47 n43, 627.
48 n43, 696.
49 n46, 292.
50 <https://www.who.int/health-topics/adolescent-health#tab=tab_1, last accessed 09/04/2023>.
51 n43, 696.
52 K. Cunningham 'Advances in juvenile adjudicative competence: A 10-year update' (2020) *Behav. Sci. Law* 38, 406, 414.
53 n46, 284.
54 n46, 284.

a deeper understanding of the development that typically occurs during childhood and adolescence, including how it affects how young people think and behave.

Arthur has argued that the standard required for effective participation is unlikely to be achievable for many young defendants because a significant proportion of children and young people are likely to experience participation difficulties due to their age and relative biological immaturity.[55] This claim is supported by the growing body of neuroscientific literature concerning brain development in children and young people, which demonstrates that developmental immaturity detrimentally affects their understanding, reasoning, reward sensitivity, time orientation, peer influence, risk perception, suggestibility, emotional responsiveness, impulsivity, abstract thinking, stability of values, perceived autonomy, and self-regulation abilities.[56]

Furthermore, scholars argue that developmentally immature derived cognitive deficits may be amplified in stressful situations, such as appearing in court.[57] Developmental immaturity can also impair a young person's ability to understand legal processes, appreciate the significance of legal circumstances for their defence, effectively communicate information to their lawyers, and exercise reasoning and judgment in making decisions as defendants.[58] These findings are significant because they demonstrate that a young person's ability to exercise cognitive and socio-emotional abilities required for effective participation may be impeded by developmental immaturity, discussed earlier in this chapter.

Research findings show that a significant proportion of children and young people, especially those under the age of 16, cannot competently participate in their own trial, regardless of whether trial proceedings occur in an adult or youth court.[59] Children and young people aged 14 to 15 are more likely to be significantly impaired in their reasoning and understanding when compared to young people aged 16 or above. Furthermore, young people aged 15 and below are more likely to endorse decisions that comply with what an authority figure may want.[60] Research has indicated that they "are more willing than adults to confess to authority figures such as police, rather than remaining silent, especially

---

55 n19, 232.
56 S. LaVelle Ficke, K. J. Hart, P. A. Deardorff 'The Performance of Incarcerated Juveniles on the MacArthur Competence Assessment Tool-Criminal Adjudication (MacCAT-CA)' (2006) 34 *The Journal of the American Academy of Psychiatry and the Law* 360, 370.
57 n52, 415.
58 T. Grisso, T et al 'Juveniles' competence to stand trial: A comparison of adolescents' and adults' capacities as trial defendants' (2003) 27 *Law & Human Behavior* 333.
59 n44,445. See also n58, 356 and Mercurio, n46, 627.
60 n58

if they believe it will result in an immediate reward, such as going home" compared to adults.[61] They were also significantly less likely to recognise the inherent risks associated with decisions and were less likely to comprehend the long-term consequences of their decisions. Such findings demonstrate that developmental immaturity is not only a factor which can cause or contribute to participation difficulties but also that a significant proportion of young defendants are likely not sufficiently developed to participate effectively in criminal proceedings.

In Grisso's research, a fifth of 14 to 15-year-olds and a third of 11 to 13-year-olds were as impaired in capacities relevant to effective adjudicative participation as seriously mentally ill adults who would likely be considered incompetent to stand trial by clinicians.[62] Although the legal concept of adjudicative competence is distinct from the concept of effective participation, there is a significant overlap between the two concepts and *SC*'s test for effective participation encapsulates the abilities required for adjudicative competence. These findings, therefore, indicate that developmental immaturity can constitute a barrier to effective participation. The findings also show that developmental immaturity profoundly impacts those under 13, meaning such children are particularly prone to experience participatory difficulties. Children in this age group are much more likely to be significantly impaired in understanding and reasoning.[63]

Overall, findings indicate that a sizeable proportion of children and young people are likely to face severe participatory difficulties because of their developmental immaturity. Research also reveals that young defendants will require additional assistance to meet the necessary participatory standard for effective participation in a criminal trial. A study of 20 young defendants found that 20% were assessed as capable of effectively participating at trial with few or no modifications.[64] In contrast, 70% were identified with significant difficulties but were deemed able to participate, provided that appropriate support and special measures were available.[65] 10% were considered unable to participate in their trial, even with significant modifications to their proceedings.[66] This highlights the need to

---

61 n43, 711.
62 n19. see also T. Grisso, 'What We Know About Youths' Capacities as Trial Defendants' in T. Grisso & R. G. Schwartz. (Eds.), *Youth on trial: A developmental perspective on juvenile justice* (University of Chicago Press, Chicago, IL, 2000) 139–171.
63 n58
64 K. Johnston et al, 'Assessing effective participation in vulnerable juvenile defendants' (2016) 27(6) *The Journal of Forensic Psychiatry & Psychology*, 802, 809.
65 n64.
66 n64, 809.

create an effective framework to properly determine the extent to which young defendants can effectively participate in their own trials.

Neuroscientific research suggests that a significant proportion of young defendants lack the capacities required to participate effectively in a trial which, in most cases, will have a significant bearing on the trajectory of their lives. This is especially the case for young defendants under the age of 14. Research demonstrates that children and young people are more likely to experience participation difficulties when compared to adults by virtue of their biological developmental immaturity.[67] This problem is further compounded by the greater prevalence of psychiatric disorders and learning disabilities or difficulties amongst the young people who offend.[68] This research "provides powerful and tangible evidence that some youths facing criminal charges may function less capably as criminal defendants than do their adult counterparts."[69] It also demonstrates that special measures and modifications are often necessary to ensure young defendants can effectively participate. Hence, there is a need for adequate legal safeguards to ensure that a child or young person's participation issues are identified and, where possible, addressed. McKeever has explained that failure to identify and appropriately address participatory barriers undermines effective participation.[70] A failure to implement effective mechanisms to ensure that participatory barriers are identified and addressed would fail to acknowledge and remove key barriers to participation faced by young defendants. This would, in turn, render the participation of many young defendants 'non-participatory' or 'tokenistic,' undermining their right to effective participation guaranteed by Article 6 of the ECHR.

4.5 Deficiencies in the Existing Legal Frameworks

Effective participation requires a defendant to exercise a wide range of cognitive and socio-emotional abilities. A defendant may face participatory difficulties due to a mental disorder, learning disability, physical disorder or disability, developmental immaturity, or a combination of these factors. The law recognises that young defendants are, by virtue of their age, vulnerable and may require assistance to enable them to participate in proceedings effectively. As such, the court is required to take "every reasonable step" to facilitate the participation of young defendants.[71] This

67 n24, para 7.35.
68 n64, 881. See also n24, para 7.39.
69 n44, 441.
70 n29, 71.
71 CrimPD 3D.3 and CrimPR 3.8(3)(a), (b) and CrimPR 3.9(3)(a) and (b).

includes enabling a defendant to give their best evidence, comprehend the proceedings, and engage fully with his or her defence. The pre-trial and trial process should, so far as necessary, be adapted to meet those ends.[72] The court may utilise any of the special measures or modifications available under the Criminal Procedure Rules (Crim PR) and the Criminal Practice Directions (Crim PD) to promote and facilitate the effective participation of young defendants. There are, however, several issues with the current legal framework that weaken the realisation of effective participation for young defendants.

Although effective participation is not a legally defined concept, "elements of it can be drawn from the jurisprudence around Article 6 that identifies – retrospectively – when effective participation has been blocked."[73] Thus, there is a conceptual issue with the realisation of effective participation and it is unsurprising that the Law Commission found that the concept has not been understood and applied consistently in practice.[74] There is also a lack of clarity as to when judges or others should act or pre-emptively take steps to secure participation.[75] Taken collectively, this all supports the formulation of a clear list of relevant capabilities, such as the one proposed by the Law Commission, "which could ensure that the concept of effective participation is understood and can be applied with the certainty and consistency that is currently lacking."[76] "A clearer statement of what the legal right to effective participation entails is necessary, not only to achieve legal certainty, but because, in practice, many defendants who are fit to plead" are not meaningfully engaged in their trials.[77] The development of such a statement or list would also enable neuroscientific researchers to undertake further research into young defendants' capacity to meet the legal threshold for effective participation. The utilisation of special measures and modifications to secure effective participation is also contingent upon participation issues being identified in the first place. As discussed above, this is particularly problematic in the summary courts because there is no coherent procedure for identifying participation issues. As Arthur has observed, "in light of the low age of criminal responsibility in England and Wales, the absence of a statutory procedure to consider a young defendant's capacity for effective participation represents a fundamental deficiency of the youth justice system."[78]

72 CrimPD 3D.3.
73 n29, 7.
74 n24, para 7.31.
75 n29,7.
76 n3, 330.
77 n3, 330.
78 n39, 232.

In some cases, barriers to participation may not be identified by the youth court and, to apply McKeever's ladder of participation, this means that the participation of some young defendants is likely to be non-participatory or tokenistic.[79] This issue is likely to be exacerbated in cases where young defendants do not have a legal representative to identify and raise participation issues.[80] As McEwan has argued, even when a young defendant is represented, the focus on delivering "swift" justice can reduce opportunities for a defendant's representatives to gain an understanding of, and raise as an issue, their lack of capacity for effective participation.[81]

Despite the growing evidence to suggest that participation issues are particularly prevalent in the young defendant population, the lack of a consistent process for identifying and raising participation issues in the youth court remains a serious cause for concern. The Law Commission has proposed that screening of all young defendants under the age of 18 for participation difficulties should take place and could help address these participation problems. The Law Commission has reasoned, "the screening process should address the defendant's capacity to participate effectively in trial generally, encompassing issues which may arise as a result of mental health difficulties, learning disability, developmental disorders and developmental immaturity."[82] Mindful of the resource implications of implementing mandatory screening for all defendants under 18, it recommended that mandatory screening should, at the very least, be implemented for all defendants under 14 appearing in the youth court for the first time. Implementing such a screening programme would help ensure participation difficulties are identified in a timely manner; thus, the court can consider which modifications may be employed to enable a young defendant's effective participation in trial proceedings at the earliest opportunity.

In *R v D*, for example, the court recognised that modifications and special measures can significantly determine whether a defendant can participate effectively in their trials.[83] Modifications may include ground rules hearings to determine the appropriate treatment of vulnerable defendants, adjustments to style and approaches to questioning, court adaptations, frequent breaks, the appointment of an intermediary, and

---

79 n43, 7.
80 n24, para 7.31.
81 J. McEwan, 'Vulnerable defendants and the fairness of trials' (2013) *Criminal Law Review* 100.
     n24, para 7.130
82 n24, para 7.130.
83 *R v D* [2013] EWCA Crim 465.

some limited provision for defendants to give evidence through live-link.[84] When appropriately utilised, the use of special measures and modifications may enable young defendants to effectively participate in proceedings,[85] although, as Owusu-Bempah has highlighted, "while special measures and trial adjustments . . . can no doubt assist participation in many cases, there is a lack of empirical research as to their effectiveness. Thus, the value of trial adjustments and special measures in individual cases may be speculative."[86]

Therefore, research needs to be undertaken to evaluate the extent to which special measures and modifications enable effective participation, particularly in the case of developmentally immature young defendants. Such research would help to identify which special measures and modifications are likely to address the types of participatory barriers caused or compounded by a young defendant's developmental immaturity. This would, in turn, enable judges to implement the most appropriate effective measures and modifications to secure the effective participation of young defendants. Such research could also inform the development of future policy. For example, research may demonstrate the extent to which particular modifications or special measures can address participatory barriers and enable policymakers to identify whether a statutory right to particular modifications or measures should be implemented.

Even when participation issues are identified, some modifications or special measures may need to go further to enable effective participation. For example, effective communication underpins several requirements for effective participation. Several of the competencies associated with effective participation require a defendant to be able to follow and understand what witnesses, judges, and lawyers say before and during court proceedings, as well as require a defendant to be able to understand and respond to questions and communicate effectively with their legal representative(s). However, many vulnerable defendants face communication difficulties. At present, this is addressed through an intermediary's appointment to assess a young defendant's communication needs and facilitate communication during proceedings. Intermediaries are, therefore, "an important resource in supporting young people's participation in a criminal trial."[87]

However, young defendants do not have a statutory or common law right to an intermediary. Instead, there is a two-tier system, with access

---

84 Criminal Practice Directions 2015 Division I: General matters (consolidated with amendment no11) [2020] EWCA Crim 1347, CrimPD 3D.

85 *R v Walls* (2011) EWCA Crim 443 at 37.

86 n3, 336.

87 R. Arthur, T. Crofts, 'The Use of Intermediaries for Young Defendants: Overcoming Barriers to Young People's Participation in Criminal Proceedings' (2022) 34 (2) *Child and Family Law Quarterly*, 149.

to the support of an intermediary determined by whether the intermediary is supporting a witness or a defendant. Arthur and Crofts argue that when "it comes to supporting a young defendant's participation in a criminal trial, the availability of support provided by an intermediary is significantly diminished."[88] This is because intermediaries appointed for defendants are private-sector intermediaries. Their role is typically limited to supporting a defendant to give evidence at trial. The support they provide does not typically extend far enough to aid a defendant's communication and comprehension throughout the whole of proceedings.[89] The appointment of defendant intermediaries while the defendant gives evidence are rare, and appointment for the duration of a trial are considered extremely rare.[90]

On the other hand, vulnerable witnesses are entitled to the assistance of a registered intermediary. These intermediaries are professionally approved, registered, and employed by the Ministry of Justice (MoJ), as well as paid by the police or by the Crown Prosecution Service.

Although young defendants are deemed vulnerable, they may not benefit from the same access to support from intermediaries as vulnerable witnesses. Arthur and Crofts argue that "all young people involved in a criminal trial, whether as a witness or an accused, should have the same right to an intermediary throughout the duration of their involvement in a criminal trial."[91] Thus, given that effective communication is an important aspect of effective participation, access to the support of a registered intermediary should be extended to young defendants.

4.6 Conclusions

The right to effective participation is a key procedural right afforded to defendants in England and Wales. It is an aspect of the right to a fair trial, which is protected by Article 6 of the ECHR and helps ensure that defendants are given a fair opportunity to answer charges brought against them. Although young defendants are considered vulnerable, and courts are obliged to take every reasonable step to facilitate the participation of young defendants, the current legal framework fails to safeguard young defendants' rights to effective participation adequately.

88 n87, 149.
89 n8, 149.
90 *TI v Bromley Youth Court* [2020] EWHC 1204 (Admin). See also Criminal Practice Directions 2015 [2015] EWCA Crim 1567, consolidated with Amendment No 1 [2016] EWCA Crim 97, [3F.3].
91 n87, 150.

Neuroscientific research strongly indicates that young defendants are, by virtue of natural biological immaturity, prone to experience participatory difficulties. Such research is invaluable as it illustrates that many of the abilities typically associated with the capacity for effective participation may be impaired by natural developmental immaturity. The existing research also reveals that some age groups, for example, those under the age of 14, are particularly prone to participatory difficulties. This research clearly demonstrates the prevalence of participatory difficulties in children and young people. It highlights the pressing need for a coherent and effective system that identifies and addresses the participatory difficulties many young defendants encounter.

This chapter has argued that, at present, the legal framework for identifying, assessing, and addressing young defendants' capacity for effective participation is inadequate. The fact that many young defendants appear before the youth court, which is specifically designed to accommodate the needs of children and young people, does not in itself ensure that they can effectively participate in criminal proceedings. This chapter has outlined some of the ways in which the legal framework for securing the effective participation of young defendants could be improved.

Neuroscientific research also provides valuable insight into the ways in which age and developmental immaturity are likely to impact a defendant's ability to participate in legal proceedings effectively. Despite this, it has not been used to inform policy development. This suggests that those involved in proceedings often do not necessarily understand or appreciate the types of participatory barriers that young defendants are likely to encounter. Consequently, they may not be able to identify or remove such barriers. This contention is supported by research demonstrating that juvenile competency evaluations often overlook adolescent development.[92] There is an opportunity for neuroscientific research to contribute to policymakers' understanding of how young defendants may encounter participatory difficulties and how such barriers to effective participation could be overcome.

Neuroscientific research should be used to inform future policy development. Research demonstrates that children and young people under 14 are more likely to be considered developmentally immature and more likely to experience participatory issues. It is, therefore, appropriate for policymakers to implement more robust safeguards for children in this age group. For example, a measure requiring all young defendants under

92 C. M. Berryessa, J. Reeves, 'The Perceptions of Juvenile Judges Regarding Adolescent Development in Evaluating Juvenile Competency' (2020) 110(3) *Journal of Criminal Law and Criminology* 551.

the age of 14 to be screened for participation issues could be justified because research shows that this age group is most likely to face participation difficulties.

There is also scope for further neuroscientific research to be undertaken to enable policymakers to understand better relationships between brain development and capacity for effective participation. For example, research which draws together normative data concerning the typical neurodevelopment of children and young people and its impact on the capacity for effective participation, particularly if such research was based on the legal concept as applied in English law, would be invaluable. Furthermore, research evaluating the extent to which special measures and modifications effectively manage or overcome participation issues would be valuable. Such research would help to identify which measures are most effective in removing or reducing barriers to participation. Thus, advances in these key areas would significantly enhance a revised legal framework, which would better safeguard young defendants' rights to effective participation.

5 Criminal Insanity in Norwegian Law between Care and Societal Protection

Sofia Moratti

5.1 The "Medical Model" of Legal Insanity and its Recent Reform

5.1.1 Continuity and Change in the 2020 Reform

In Norway, the insanity clause was last reformed in 2020.[1] Section 20 of the Norwegian Penal Code currently in force regulates "criminal capacity" (*skyldevne*).[2] The second paragraph in the provision exonerates the offender "who at the time of the act is unaccountable due to" one of the following conditions: "severely deviant state of mind," "severely impaired consciousness," or "severe mental disability." According to Norwegian legal doctrine, the first of the three conditions listed is the insanity clause proper.[3] There is no diminished responsibility clause in Norwegian law.[4] Section 20 also stipulates that, in the assessment, "emphasis shall be given to the degree of failure in the person's perception of reality and functional capacity."[5]

---

1 LOV-2019-06-21-48 Law of 21 June 2019 nr. 48, *Act on Amendments to the Penal Code and the Criminal Procedure Act (Criminal Capacity, Societal Protection and Forensic Expertise).* The law came into force in 2020.
2 LOV-2005-05-20-28 Law of 20 May 2005 nr. 28, *Penal Code.* An official English translation is available at <https://lovdata.no/dokument/NLE/lov/2005-05-20-28> (accessed 25 April 2023).
3 This is a narrower definition of "legal insanity" (*galskap*) compared to other countries. See L. Gröning, 'Criminal Insanity in Norwegian Law' in R. Mackay, W. Brookbanks, (eds), *The Insanity Defence. International and Comparative Perspectives* (OUP, Oxford 2022), C12.P2. Available at <https://academic.oup.com/book/45347/chapter/389264838> (accessed 2 May 2023).
4 Ibid, C13.P4.
5 Section (§) 20 of the Penal Code (post-2020 version, official English translation). "Accountability (*Skyldevne*)
A person who at the time of the act is under 15 years old, is not criminally liable (*strafferettslig ansvarlig*).
The same applies to a person who at the time of the act is unaccountable (*utilregnelig*) due to a

DOI: 10.4324/9781003331056-6

Before the 2020 reform, the phrasing of the insanity clause was much more succinct. There was no requirement in the law that unaccountability must be "due to" the person's condition. Nor was there mention of "failure in the person's perception of reality and functional capacity."[6] The old phrasing of the clause had attracted criticism for giving forensic psychiatrists too prominent a role in legal insanity determinations.[7] The legal change goes toward creating more room for judicial discretion in what is, after all, a primarily legal assessment.

The extent to which the 2020 reform otherwise departs from the Norwegian criminal law tradition is debated.[8] Norway is often cited for its "*pure* medical model" of legal insanity, which dates back to 1929[9] and runs counter to the insanity doctrines of most countries.[10] "Medical model" means that the law *equates* criminal insanity with some mental

---

- severely deviant state of mind (*sterkt avvikende sinnstilstand*)
- severely impaired consciousness or
- severe mental disability.

When assessing unaccountability pursuant to the second paragraph, emphasis shall be given to the degree of failure in the person's perception of reality and functional capacity (*graden av svikt i virkelighetsforståelse og funksjonsevne.*)"

The final paragraph in the provision regulates self-induced intoxication and it is not relevant for the purposes of the present Chapter.

6 § 20 of the Penal Code (pre-2020 version). "Accountability (*Tilregnelighet*).

In order to be punishable, the offender must be accountable at the time of the act. The offender is not accountable if he is at the time of the act

1. Below the age of 15,
2. Psychotic (*psykotisk*),
3. Mentally disabled to a high degree
4. Severely consciousness-impaired."

The final paragraph in the provision regulates self-induced intoxication and it is not relevant for the purposes of the present Chapter.

7 L. Gröning and G.F. Rieber-Mohn, 'NOU 2014:10 - Proposal for New Rules Regarding Criminal Insanity and Related Issues, Norway post-22 July' (2015) 3 *Bergen Journal of Criminal Law and Criminal Justice* 109, 112.

8 R. Rosenqvist, 'The Insanity Defence: How Do We Handle Doubt?' (2019) 7(1) *Bergen Journal of Criminal Law & Criminal Justice* 60, 61.

9 However, Gröning et al contend that already the 1842 Norwegian Penal Code was "to a certain extent" based on the medical model. See L. Gröning, U. K. Hansen Haukvik, and K. H. Melle 'Criminal Insanity, Psychosis and Impaired Reality Testing in Norwegian Law' (2019) 7 *Bergen Journal of Criminal Law & Criminal Justice* 27, 32. For a comprehensive history of legal insanity in Norway, see S. A. Skålevåg, 'The Irresponsible Criminal in Norwegian Medico-legal Discourse' (2014) 37(1) *International Journal of law and psychiatry* 82.

10 C-F. Stuckenberg, 'Comparing Legal Approaches: Mental Disorders as Grounds for Excluding Criminal Responsibility' (2016) 4 *Bergen Journal of Criminal Law and Criminal Justice* 48, 52 and G. Meynen, *Legal Insanity: Explorations in Psychiatry, Law, and Ethics* (Springer, Cham, 2016) 35.

disorder "at the time of the act"[11] and requires no proof that the disorder causally influenced the commission of the crime (such a proof would instead be required under a "mixed model" of legal insanity). As that central feature of the "medical model" was left untouched by the 2020 reform,[12] some legal scholars contend that "failure in the perception of reality and functional capacity" must be understood as referring to the severity of the disorder, not to its influence on the crime.[13] However, in the legislative proposal leading up to the 2020 reform, the Norwegian Ministry of Justice stated that the legal change marks the transition to a "*modified* mixed model;" indeed, while the mental disorder remains central ("basic condition"), the offender should also be deemed "unaccountable" ("limiting condition").[14]

5.1.2 *"Psychosis" and Legal Insanity*

The Norwegian insanity clause had already been reformed before 2020. However, the "medical model" had remained the dominant paradigm "operationalized in Norwegian law through different statutory rules."[15] The evolution in the lexical choices made by the legislator is of special interest here. In the 1929 phrasing of the clause, the word "insane" was used (*sinnssyk*, now a dated term). In 2002, the word "insane" was replaced with "psychotic" (*psykotisk*), creating a *direct* connection with the medical-nosographic category:[16] "psychosis" at the time of the act

---

11 "At the time of the act" means that "it is the condition when the crime was committed and not the formal diagnosis that results in acquittal" (see supra Rosenqvist 2019, 73). In other words, it is "not sufficient for the perpetrator to have a diagnosis" (see supra Gröning et al 2019, 36). The mental disorder must be "discernible at the time of the offence through obvious symptoms" (see supra Gröning 2022, C13.P12).

12 As stated in the legislative proposal leading up to the 2020 reform: "What is decisive is that the offender was insane while committing the offence, not that he committed the offence because he was insane." Prop 154 L (2016–2017) *Amendments to the Penal Code and the Criminal Procedure Act (Criminal Capacity, Societal Protection and Forensic Expertise*, 13. My translation.

13 See supra Gröning (2022), C13.P61.

14 See supra Prop 154 L (2016–2017), 13. My translation. Nonetheless, some legal scholars have argued that the departure from the medical model is much smaller than it appears, and "the severity of the psychosis will remain central". See L. Gröning et al, 'Constructing Criminal Insanity: The Roles of Legislators, Judges and Experts in Norway, Sweden and the Netherlands' (2020) 11 *New Journal of European Criminal Law* 390, 398.

15 L. Gröning et al, 'Remodelling Criminal Insanity: Exploring Philosophical, Legal, and Medical Premises of the Medical Model used in Norwegian Law' (2022) 81 *International Journal of Law and Psychiatry* 1, 3.

16 LOV-1997-01-17-11 Law of 17 January 1997, nr. 11. *Act on Amendments to the Penal Code (Criminal Insanity Rules and Special Reactions)*. The law came into force in 2002.

was effectively treated as "a proxy for insanity."[17] Critics have argued that "law tends to confuse the proxy with the things proxied. . . Norwegian (insanity) law takes too seriously the distinctly medical conceptualizations of psychosis."[18] "The criteria of *legal* responsibility are for the *law* to settle,"[19] and concepts developed by the medical profession for medical purposes, such as "psychosis," should not be imported into the law and used for legal purposes. The goal of the law in theorising legal insanity is to create a concept that "captures all and only those who are excused morally and then legally."[20] Disease prevention, treatment, or even the accurate scientific description of pathologies that exist in nature are not among the law's goals. The law does not seek to explain the person's condition, but to *evaluate* whether the condition interfered with responsibility for behaviour. However, legal scholars have argued that, terminological identity aside, "the judicial concept of psychosis was narrower than the medical concept" as the former only encompassed psychotic symptoms above a certain threshold of severity.[21] The 2020 phrasing of the clause, "severely deviant state of mind", does not draw from medical terminology; that lexical change goes, again, in the direction of expanding the role of the judge in insanity assessments.

A related question is what "psychosis" effectively means in forensic practice. There is relatively little information available on operationalising the pre-2020 "medical model" in concrete psychiatric evaluations. To substantiate an insanity defence, the psychosis had to be "discernible at the time of the offence through obvious symptoms."[22] There are no official statistics for all insanity trials in Norway, but they are relatively few: according to experts, less than 250 per year.[23] Gröning and colleagues conducted a pilot study of all legal insanity cases published between January 2013 and November 2018 in the Norwegian national database *lovdata*. The study indicates that insanity verdicts were often associated with psychiatric diagnoses (mainly schizophrenia) and psychotic

---

17 Gröning et al (2022), at p. 1. See also I. Melle, 'The Breivik case and what psychiatrists can learn from it.' (2013) 12 *World Psychiatry* 16, 17.

18 M. S. Moore, 'The Quest for a Responsible Responsibility Test: Norwegian Insanity Law after Breivik' 9 (2015) *Criminal Law and Philosophy* 645, 689. See also supra Meynen (2016), 36.

19 M. S. Moore, 'Legal Conceptions of Mental Illness' in B. Brody, J. Engelhardt (eds), *Mental Illness: Law and Public Policy, Philosophy and Medicine* (D. Reidel, Dordrecht, 1980) 25, 36 (my Italics).

20 See supra Moore (2015), 657.

21 A. Løvlie, 'Criminal Insanity: Concepts and Evidence.' (2019) 7 *Bergen Journal of Criminal Law & Criminal Justice* 78, 82.

22 See supra Gröning et al (2020), 393.

23 See supra Gröning et al (2022), 4.

symptomatology (primarily hallucinations and delusions).[24] Interestingly, studies from other countries that do not adopt the "medical model" of insanity show similar patterns.[25] That factual similarity may be because "hallucinations and delusions are the positive core symptoms in impaired reality testing, and schizophrenia is the disorder in which they most often occur."[26] Boundaries between legal models appear more clear-cut on a doctrinal and legal-theoretical level but are more nuanced at the empirical, forensic-practice level. Prominent scholars have argued that the centrality of psychosis in the "insanity judgments in most countries" makes it the "common core of the Western idea of criminal incapacity."[27]

The process of legal change in Norway leading to the 2020 insanity reform was triggered by the high-profile *Breivik* trial.[28] The trial is well-known internationally as it concerns a case of politically motivated terrorism of exceptional magnitude and severity. The perpetrator received two legal insanity assessments during the trial, each reaching *opposite* conclusions. This was a paradoxical outcome, especially considering that the Norwegian legislator has historically invoked legal certainty as the rationale for adopting the "medical model," which compresses judicial discretion in favour of "science;" the "medical model" is the child of positivism and societal defence-centred criminal justice theories.[29] In Norway, *Breivik* was accompanied and followed by very lively public, political, and intra-professional debates among law scholars and forensic psychiatrists on the regulation of criminal insanity, the role of the expert witness in insanity determinations, the regulation of forensic psychiatry as a profession, and the role of criminal outcomes aimed to dangerous offenders with an insanity verdict (such as compulsory care orders). *Breivik* is presented below with the concomitant and subsequent debates and legal developments, some of which affect vulnerable mentally ill defendants and security-psychiatry patients, despite having originated from understandable societal-protection concerns in the aftermath of a politically motivated mass murder, perpetrated by a terrorist who was eventually found to be of sound mind.

---

24 See supra Gröning et al (2019).
25 M. L. Perlin, 'The Insanity Defense: Nine Myths That Will Not Go Away'. In M. D. White (Ed), *The Insanity Defense: Multidisciplinary Views on its History, Trends and Controversies* (Praeger, California, 2017), 7 and G. Tsimploulis et al, 'Schizophrenia and Criminal Responsibility' (2018) 206 *The Journal of Nervous and Mental Disease* 370.
26 See supra Gröning et al (2022), 4.
27 See supra Gröning et al (2019), 28.
28 TOSLO-2011-188627-24 Oslo District Court, Judgment of 24 August 2012. Available in English at <https://lovdata.no/static/file/1282/toslo-2011-188627-24-eng.pdf> (last accessed 3 April 2023).
29 See supra Gröning et al (2019), 34. See also supra Skålevåg (2014), 87.

5.2 The *Breivik* Case

5.2.1 The *"Lone Wolf" Terrorist Who Had Radicalised Online*

On 22 July 2011, the far-right extremist Anders Behring Breivik – a private citizen previously unknown to the Norwegian media – murdered 77 people in two unprovoked and planned attacks. The first attack was a car bombing in the government quarters of the city of Oslo. The 950 kg bomb that he used was rudimentary and made with fertiliser. Breivik subsequently reached the island of Utøya, where hundreds of youngsters were gathered for the yearly Labour Party youth camp. Passing as a policeman – dressed in a uniform complete with a bulletproof vest, forged badge, and armed with a pistol and a hunting rifle – he approached the camp coordinators and opened fire. The mass-shooting left 69 dead and another 66 wounded; most victims were teenagers. Breivik was arrested about an hour after he first opened fire. He was unharmed and did not oppose resistance. He stated that his deeds had been politically motivated. He had meticulously planned and carried out the attacks alone: he was a "lone wolf terrorist" who had radicalised online.[30] He was put in pre-trial custody on counts of terrorism, with both visitation and media bans. The attacks created a wave of shock among the Norwegian public. There had been only a few precedents of politically motivated, far-right violent attacks in Norway in the late 1970s and mid-1980s, but of a much smaller magnitude.[31]

5.2.2 Assessed as Insane: The *Sørheim-Husby* Report and the Debate That Followed

Following the standard procedure for competency assessments in criminal trials, Breivik was examined by two reputable forensic psychiatrists appointed by the Oslo District Court as expert witnesses.[32] They used traditional methods of psychiatric investigation – mainly conversations with the defendant (12 discussions for 35 hours). In November 2011, they delivered a 243-page report (known as the *Sørheim-Husby* report), which is an exceptionally extensive assessment, considering that such reports are "usually 30–40 pages long."[33] The experts concluded that Breivik was psychotic at the time of the

---

30 A. Dafnos, 'Lone Wolf Terrorism as Category: Learning from the Breivik Case' (2013) 3 *Journal EXIT-Deutschland. Zeitschrift für Deradikalisierung und Demokratische Kultur* 96, 102.

31 A. Syse, 'Breivik–the Norwegian terrorist case' (2014) 32 *Behavioral Sciences & the Law* 389, 391–392.

32 Ibid, 399.

33 See supra Gröning (2022), C13.P8.

crime and legally insane. They issued a diagnosis of paranoid schizophrenia. His "most implausible beliefs" were regarded as "bizarre delusions," such as his claim of being the leader of a "Knights Templar" organization (which did not exist, according to the Norwegian police).[34] The *Sørheim-Husby* report was reviewed by the National Board on Forensic Medicine, as is standard practice in competency assessments, and it was approved in December 2011. The media later reported that, during the discussion of the report by the Board, some Board members had voiced their disagreement.[35]

This assessment was challenged by the mental health professionals who treated Breivik while he was in custody. One of them was a renowned forensic psychiatrist and former leader of the National Board of Forensic Medicine. In her capacity as the Prison Medical Officer (and upon request of the prison Director), she had delivered her assessment of Breivik a few months earlier and concluded that he was not psychotic.[36] In an often-cited interview with the German magazine *Der Spiegel*, she pointed out that "for historical reasons. . . there is a tradition of caution when it comes to diagnosing mental illness in cases involving politically motivated perpetrators." For example, she said that "nobody would have even thought" of declaring the Baader-Meinhof gang terrorists "incapable of guilt." As a counterexample, she referred to the widespread abuse of psychiatric diagnoses for political dissidents in the Soviet Union.[37] The *Sørheim-Husby* assessment, as well as the confidential reports by the Prison Medical Officer, were leaked to the press; this added fuel to the fire of an already feverish public debate.[38]

5.2.3 *Methodological Questions and Legal Certainty: Diagnostic Guidelines, Scoring Systems and "Neuroskepticism"*

The diagnosis of paranoid schizophrenia was questioned by other prominent mental health experts, who argued that a conclusion for legal insanity was unwarranted.[39] The National Board of Forensic Medicine

---

34 L. Bortolotti, M. R. Broome, M. Mameli, 'Delusions and Responsibility for Action: Insights from the Breivik Case' (2014) 7 *Neuroethics* 377.

35 J. Sætre, A. Moland, 'Psykiaterne i full splid om Breiviks helsetilstand' [Psychiatrists in complete disagreement about Breivik's health condition]. NRK, 21.12.2011.

36 See supra Syse (2014), 400.

37 The Baader-Meinhof gang, also known as the Red Army Faction, carried out a series of deadly bombings and assassinations in Germany between the 1970s and 1990s. G. Traufetter, 'Experts Disagree on Psychological State of Norwegian Killer' *Spiegel International*, 23.12.2011.

38 See supra Syse (2014), 400.

39 P-A. Johansen and A. Bakke Foss, 'Eksperter tviler på grunnlaget for Behring Breiviks diagnose' [Experts question the basis for Behring Breivik's diagnosis]. Aftenposten, 04.12.2011.

requires that experts rely on the diagnostic criteria set forth in the most recent edition of the ICD manual by the WHO ("International Statistical Classification of Diseases and Related Health Problems" by the World Health Organization). Aside from that requirement, the Board offers no specific diagnostic guidelines for forensic practice. The Board monitors all insanity assessments for quality assurance, while the National Network for Security-, Prison- and Forensic-Psychiatry (SIFER) organizes courses for forensic mental health professionals.[40] Nonetheless, in forensic practice, multiple diagnostic approaches coexist to this day.[41] The mental-health assessment tools available to clinicians and, in principle, relevant to an insanity assessment are many; part of the intra-professional discussion during *Breivik* focused on divergent interpretations of how and when to use psychiatric assessment scales and scoring systems.[42] Most psychological and psychiatric assessment tools have been developed in treatment or research settings and there is no intra-professional consensus on whether to use such tests in insanity assessments and which tests to use.[43] Research shows that such tools are often not used in forensic evaluations of criminal responsibility in Norway. Løvgren and colleagues examined 500 reports filed with the Norwegian Board of Forensic Medicine in 2009–2018 for defendants indicted for the most serious violent crimes. They found that assessment tools were used in half the reports overall, although their use increased during the study period.[44]

As is established practice in criminal courts all over Europe, such tools often consist of structured tests and interview guides, but do not usually include brain imaging. This widespread "neuroskepticism,"[45] which is well-documented in comparative studies across jurisdictions and especially in Europe,[46] aligns with the cautious attitudes of scientists investigating

---

40 SIFER is a network created in 2011, a collaboration between the Norwegian Regional Research and Education Centra for Security-, Prison- and Forensic Psychiatry. At that time, the Regional Centra based in Oslo, Bergen and Trondheim had existed for over a decade: see St. Meld. nr. 25 (1996–97), 106–107.
41 See supra Gröning et al (2020), 395-396. See also supra Gröning et al (2019), 42.
42 One example is the intra-professional debate on the use of the Global Assessment of Functioning scale (GAF), which had been used by Sørheim and Husby. See G.A. Feigum Pedersen, 'Global funksjonsskåring – like aktuelt etter siste versjon av diagnosesystemet DSM.' [GAF – just as relevant after the latest version of the diagnostic system DSM.] (2014) 134(9) *Tidsskrift for Den norske legeforening* 916.
43 See supra Gröning et al (2019), 42.
44 P. J. Løvgren et al, 'Use of Assessment Instruments in Forensic Evaluations of Criminal Responsibility in Norway' (2022) 22(1) *BMC Psychiatry* 235.
45 J. A. Humbach, 'Do Criminal Minds Cause Crime: Neuroscience and the Physicalism Dilemma' (2019) 12 *Washington University. Jurisprudence Review* 1, 7–8.
46 S. Moratti, D. Patterson (eds.), *Legal Insanity and the Brain: Science, Law and European Courts* (Bloomsbury, Oxford, 2016) and T. M. Spranger (ed.), *International Neurolaw. A Comparative Analysis* (Springer, Heidelberg, 2012).

the neurobiology of impulse control and psychopathy. State-of-the-art science and technology available and used today are not yet ready to make conclusive, *retrospective* inferences between brain states and criminal behaviour. Neuroscience can, at best, be used along with traditional insanity assessment techniques, but only as a "complementary and secondary" method.[47] The same caution is shared by the Norwegian scholars Fjellvang, Gröning, and Haukvik, who performed a systematic review of in-vivo MRI studies of the neurobiological underpinnings of psychotic violence (with a focus on schizophrenia). The authors concluded that such studies do have a potential to inform legal evaluations, but only in the future.[48]

The intra-professional controversy on Breivik's criminal capacity extended beyond Norway, as Danish and Swedish psychiatrists intervened. The media debate (and later, the political debate) increasingly focused on the role of expert witnesses in criminal insanity determinations. Some contended that role was excessive,[49] to the detriment of "the rule of law."[50] Be that true or not, it has been argued that "reading (Norwegian) criminal insanity judgments often leaves one wondering how the court found its way from the diagnostic evaluation…to the *legal* conclusion;" indeed, the courts' *legal* argumentation about insanity is typically "full of medical language."[51] Gröning et al compellingly argued that concepts central to insanity determinations, including "psychosis" and "reality testing," have no clear and consistent meaning – neither in Norwegian forensic practice, nor in medical science. How does one prove psychosis *retrospectively*, and how can one locate the cut-off point at which psychosis becomes severe enough to substantiate an insanity verdict? These and other crucial questions have no precise answers.[52] Thus, giving centre stage to "science," under the "medical model," does not seem to have led to a particularly high degree of legal certainty.

47 C. Korponay, M. Koenigs, 'The Neurobiology of Antisocial and Amoral Behaviour: Insights from Brain Science and Implications for Law' in S. Moratti and D. Patterson (2016), 33. See also D. L. Egbenya, S. Adjorlolo, 'Advancement of neuroscience and the assessment of mental state at the time of offense' (2021) 2 *Forensic Science International: Mind and Law* 100046, 7.

48 M. Fjellvang, L. Gröning, U. K. Haukvik, 'Imaging Violence in Schizophrenia: A Systematic Review and Critical Discussion of the MRI Literature' (2018) 9 *Frontiers in Psychiatry* 1, 8.

49 See supra Gröning et al (2019), 28.

50 I. Andersen, I. Dahl-Nilssen, E.-M. Bulai, A. Moland, 'Krever sakkyndig-revolusjon etter Breivik-saken' [Demands for a forensic expertise revolution after the *Breivik* case]. NRK, 29 February 2012.

51 See supra Gröning et al (2019), 37–38. My italics.

52 Ibid., 58.

5.2.4 *The Lex Breivik: Compulsory Care and Societal Protection*

In the event of an insanity verdict, where would Breivik go, and would he be adequately incapacitated there? That question came to the forefront of public debates, as there was apprehension about his risk for future criminality. Media speculations pointed to the Regional Security Department at one psychiatric hospital not far from Oslo.[53] Regional Security Departments are high-security psychiatry units, treatment facilities for psychiatric patients who display at-risk behaviour. Their tasks include the execution of "compulsory care" court orders for offenders determined to be legally insane.[54] Prominent criminal law scholars contend that a new law was "hastily enacted" with "a specific perpetrator in mind" right after the issuing of the *Sørheim-Husby* report (concluding for legal insanity).[55] The law added a new chapter (Chapter 4A) to the 1999 Mental Health Care Act,[56] introducing new rules for body searches of patients and visitors, room and property searches, telephone and e-mail tapping, and escape-prevention measures in Regional Security Departments. The new law came into force on 1 July 2012 and was nicknamed *Lex Breivik* for its alleged *ad personam* character.[57] The then-Minister of Health stated that the bill had been on the table for a long time, along with the need to "strengthen security" in Regional Security Departments: the *Breivik* case only gave it new relevance.[58] Whatever the motives of the legislature, the legal change affected many recipients of compulsory care orders, as well as psychiatric patients without criminal histories as Norway has no dedicated forensic-psychiatric hospitals.[59] It was met with criticism in the media

---

53 C. Wernersen, 'Dette kan bli Breiviks nye hverdag' [This could be Breivik's new everyday life]. NRK, 30 November 2011.

54 "Compulsory care", provided for in Section 62 of the Norwegian Penal Code, is at the same time medical treatment and incapacitation. It is not punishment. Under Norwegian law, punishment presupposes criminal capacity. See supra Gröning et al (2020), 394.

55 L. Gröning, 'Patient Autonomy and Criminal Law: A Norwegian perspective' in P. Daniluk (ed), *Patient Autonomy and Criminal Law: European Perspectives* (Routledge, New York, 2023) 231.

56 LOV-2012-06-22-48 Law of 22 June 2012 nr. 48, *Amendments to the Mental Health Care Act (Regional Security Departments and High-Security Units)*. The law amends LOV-1999-07-02-62 Law of 2 July 1999 nr. 62, *Act on the Establishment and Implementation of Mental Health Care (Mental Health Care Act)*.

57 In addition, the *Lex Breivik* gives the Ministry the authority to decide whether to create one Special (security-psychiatry) Unit, with an even higher level of security and significant restrictions in human rights-sensitive areas. Particularly that measure was framed in the media as being directed at Breivik. See K. Falch-Nilsen, '«Lex Breivik» kommer 1. juli' [The "Lex Breivik" is coming on July 1]. NRK, 22 June 2012.

58 Ibid.

59 See supra Gröning (2023), 231. See also A. Syse, 'Tvungent psykisk helsevern' [Compulsory care] (2016) 42 *Kritisk juss* 278.

(one critic called it "collective punishment for the mentally ill")[60] and in Parliament. One MP contended that the *Lex Breivik* granted a *de facto* "blank power of attorney" to medical practitioners, who are invested with the authority to decide on searches and restrictions[61] – suggesting the law "belongs. . . to another era". The MP expressed concern for the "tone" and "basic attitude" of the debate as compared to previous parliamentary debates on "coercion in psychiatry."[62] One person unaffected by the *Lex Breivik* was Breivik himself as he eventually did not receive a compulsory care order but, rather, underwent a second legal insanity assessment that found him sane.

5.2.5 Assessed as Sane: The Aspaas-Tørrissen Report and Breivik's Conviction

Throughout his trial, Breivik was adamant that he did not wish to be seen as insane. He described himself as a political activist and was strongly critical of *Sørheim-Husby*.[63] However, he was not keen on a second psychiatric assessment. The counsel for the massacre victims and their families had petitioned the Court for a new evaluation. In early 2012, the Court appointed two new expert witnesses. Breivik, initially reluctant, eventually cooperated with them. The new assessment was again based on traditional psychiatric investigation methodologies, mainly behavioural observation carried out inside a specially built 60 square-meter prison cell (in addition to testing procedures and interviews). The new expert report (called *Aspaas-Tørrissen*), published in April 2012, concluded that Breivik did not have paranoid schizophrenia and was not "psychotic" at the time of the crime nor at the time of the examination. The conclusion was that he suffered from "antisocial personality disorder" and "narcissistic personality disorder." These diagnoses did not support a legal insanity verdict.[64] Breivik was eventually ruled sane and guilty by the Oslo District

60 A. Kirkevik, 'Breivik-paragrafane – kollektiv staff for psykisk sjuke' [The *Breivik* law – collective punishment for the mentally ill] (2012) 2 *Syn og Segn* 12.

61 The patient (and his or her next of kin) can lodge an appeal to the institutional Control Commission, regulated under Chapter 6 of the 1999 Mental Health Care Law. The Commission is chaired by a legal professional. However, in the first instance it is the medical practitioner in charge who decides on searches and restrictions.

62 Norwegian Parliament, Session of Monday 11 June 2012 at 10.00. Issue nr. 1. Transcript available at <https://www.stortinget.no/no/Saker-og-publikasjoner/Publikasjoner/Referater/Stortinget/2011-2012/120611/1> (accessed 3 April 2023).

63 See supra Melle (2013), 18.

64 See supra Syse (2014), 400–401. With its 310 pages, *Aspaas-Tørrissen* was an even longer document than *Sørheim-Husby*. See V. Buan, P-A. Holm, A. Bakke Foss, A. Færaas, 'Sakkyndige konkluderer med at Behring Breivik er tilregnelig' [The experts conclude that Behring Breivik is criminally accountable]. Aftenposten, 10.04.2012.

Court, and he was sentenced to 21 years in prison by a unanimous court in August 2012.[65] The sentence was not appealed by Breivik nor by the prosecution. The court criticised the *Sørheim-Husby* assessment (and its conclusion for legal insanity) for failing to interpret Breivik's statements in light of the subculture of which he claims to be a part:[66] beliefs that seem delusional on their face (such as Breivik's claim to be part of a civil war) can be understood as meaningful in a right-wing extremist subculture.[67] The odd neologisms he used are also borrowed from that subculture: they are not the product of his imagination and can be found on the internet.[68] Furthermore, Breivik never manifested hallucinations.[69] The "lone wolf" was sentenced as a criminally sane, politically motivated terrorist. However, the case had triggered a process of socio-legal change focused on criminal insanity, that developed further.

5.2.6 Medical-Professional Authority "on Loan"? The Role of the Media and the Public

The *Breivik* trial was followed by a lively debate on regulating legal insanity and the role of forensic psychiatrists in insanity determinations. That is not surprising. According to Gutheil, "every high-profile insanity trial since and including the M'Naghten case in England in 1843 has been followed by an outcry from the public, press and politicians for changes in the law, altered rules and sweeping reforms, as well as professional embarrassment from psychiatrists."[70] Syse detected "striking similarities between the governments' follow-ups in the M'Naghten, the Hinckley and Breivik cases".[71] Bortolotti and colleagues pointed to crucial resemblances in public debates surrounding *Breivik* and in the *London Nail Bomber* trial, involving a man who killed 3 people and injured 139 by using homemade nail bombs in 1999.[72]

---

65 Breivik was sentenced to a special form of prison sentence introduced in Norwegian law in 2001 and called "containment", "the maximum penalty in Norway" as its duration can in principle be indefinite. The court can prolong it for "successive periods of five years" if the convict is found to pose a serious threat to society. Breivik was placed in a high-security prison unit. See supra Syse (2014), 391.

66 See supra TOSLO-2011-188627-24, 103.

67 Ibid., 81.

68 C. Jacobsen, D. Maier-Katkin, 'Breivik's Sanity: Terrorism, Mass Murder, and the Insanity Defense.' (2015) 37 *Human Rights Quarterly* 137, 144.

69 See supra Bortolotti et al (2014), 378.

70 T. G. Gutheil, 'Ethics and Forensic Psychiatry' in S. Bloch and S. A. Green (eds.) (2009), *Psychiatric Ethics* (4th ed.) (Oxford: OUP) 443, 443.

71 See supra Syse (2014), 406.

72 See supra Bortolotti et al (2014), 378–379.

It is certainly true that, during the *Breivik* trial, public emotion was intense, and expert witnesses worked under considerable pressure. Forensic psychiatrists (as a professional group) were criticised in the media, for being purportedly too concerned with opaque intra-professional controversies.[73] The media got hold of and published confidential information from the expert witnesses' reports and even oral discussions in the Board of Forensic Medicine; those leaks added to the pressure. Psychiatric-ethics scholars have provocatively argued that part of the public seems to harbour an illusion of expertise when assessing mental states; some "regard themselves as sound psychologists and thus able to detect malingering from the televised image of a defendant."[74] Regardless, it is true that forensic psychiatrists and their work are subject to more public scrutiny as compared to other expert witnesses, such as geneticists. Some scholars have attributed that to preconceived lay ideas about psychiatry. When discussing the attitudes of the public during *Breivik*, the well-known psychiatrist Simon Wessely pointed to an underlying tension between a desire for retribution – rooted in the moral intuition that deeds of such magnitude cannot go unpunished – and a general sentiment that no sane person would be capable of such egregious crimes. This tension, he argued, may, in turn, be rooted in two misconceptions about psychiatry among the public: that "outrageous crimes must mean mental illness" and that "the purpose of psychiatry is to get people off."[75] In a highly politicised area of criminal justice such as legal insanity, it may be expected that public perceptions can play a critical role.[76] John Gunn, one of the expert witnesses in the *London Nail Bomber* trial, boldly argued that "the power" conferred to forensic psychiatrists in high-profile criminal trials is "on loan, and can be withdrawn when the politics of a case. . . demand it" lest the trial is followed by "a public outcry."[77] While that is a strong claim, it speaks to the intense pressure that forensic psychiatrists can experience in high-profile cases. By creating a sense of erosion to professional autonomy and authority, such pressure may exacerbate dif-

73 See supra Melle (2013), 20.

74 See supra Gutheil (2009), 443. See also supra Melle (2013), 19: "Many TV stations and newspapers used "expert commentators" focusing on Breivik's state of mind throughout the trial, sometimes attempting to discern a diagnosis based on his appearance in court."

75 S. Wessely, 'Anders Breivik, the Public, and Psychiatry' (2012) 379 *The Lancet* 1563, 1563–1564. Wessely sat in an International Advisory Council appointed by the Norwegian Government and tasked with reviewing the medical and psycho-social emergency response to the attacks perpetrated by Breivik.

76 See S. Moratti and D. Patterson, 'Introduction' in S. Moratti, D. Patterson (eds.), *Legal Insanity and the Brain: Science, Law and European Courts* (Bloomsbury, Oxford, 2016), 1.

77 Gunn argued that in the London Nail Bomber trial, the perpetrator was deemed criminally responsible, despite evidence pointing to a severe form of schizophrenia. J. Gunn, 'No excuses' (2002) 95 *Journal of the Royal Society of Medicine* 61, 62.

ferences of opinion between experts and contribute to high degrees of polarisation in intra-professional debates.

5.3 The Process of Legal Change Following the *Breivik* Case

5.3.1 Reforms of Legal Insanity and Forensic Psychiatry

In the wake of the *Breivik* trial, the former Attorney General of Norway stated that, in his 40 years of professional experience, he had never seen a disagreement of such magnitude among forensic-psychiatry expert witnesses in a legal insanity case.[78] Reforms were advocated and carried out, pursuing multiple goals: providing new rules on forensic-psychiatric professional accreditation for standardisation and quality assurance,[79] reconsidering the roles of forensic experts in insanity determinations, and providing stronger societal protection from dangerous offenders.

The Minister of Justice set up an *ad hoc* Commission that delivered its report entitled "Criminal capacity, (forensic-psychiatric) expertise and societal protection" in late 2014.[80] The Commission was multidisciplinary. Most of its members were legal experts, but it also included mental health experts, philosophers, and the leader of a national interest organisation for people with psychiatric conditions and their relatives.[81] Partly building on the conclusions in the Commission's Report, the Ministry of Justice (with the approval of the Cabinet) submitted a legislative proposal to the Norwegian Parliament in mid-2017.[82] The Commission had recommended that they preserve the "medical model" but extend it to include "conditions that are equated with psychosis."[83] The legislature

---

78 M. Vikås, E. B. Utheim, M. S. Hopperstad, 'Rieber-Mohn: – Aldri opplevd dette før' [Rieber-Mohn: I never experienced this before]. VG, 24 May 2012.

79 In the words of Kirsten Rasmussen, professor of Forensic Psychology and Member of the Norwegian Board of Forensic Psychiatry: "Norwegian forensic psychiatry is largely run as a private enterprise. There are no accepted standards for how the examinations should be carried out or where they should take place" and a "greater alignment" would benefit "equality before the law." K. Rasmussen, 'Norsk rettsmedisin ved kjøkkenbord og på parkbenker' [Norwegian forensic medicine at the kitchen table and on park benches] (2016) 136 *Tidsskrift for Den norske legeforening* 1462, 1462. My translation.

80 NOU 2014: 10. *Criminal Capacity, (Forensic-Psychiatric) Expertise and Societal Protection.* Available at https://www.regjeringen.no/no/dokumenter/NOU-2014-10/id2008986/ (accessed 3 April 2023).

81 A high degree of multi-disciplinarity was one of the goals pursued by the Government, when setting up the Committee: see Ministry of Justice, Press Release nr. 150, 30 December 2012.

82 See supra Prop 154 L (2016–2017).

83 See supra Gröning et al (2020), 397. See also supra Gröning and Rieber-Mohn (2015), 114.

chose to go one step further than the Commission in questioning the "medical model," and the eventual outcome of the reform process was the legal development described in the opening section of this chapter.

The role of forensic mental health experts in insanity evaluations was also significantly reformed. Their role is now limited to a strictly medical evaluation. Expert witnesses no longer assess whether the defendant's condition meets the criteria for insanity listed in Section 20 of the Penal Code, as doing so "required them to interpret the *legal* meaning of these criteria;"[84] nor do they assess whether the defendant was "unaccountable due to" their condition. Importantly, the experts are required to avoid using "expressions that could be confused with legal criteria." Their task is *to inform* the court as to the defendant's medical condition and his or her "degree of failure in the perception of reality and functional capacity." The eventual decision on legal insanity rests with the court alone.[85] As this reform is quite recent, it is still too early to assess its effect on legal practice, but such a study will certainly be of great interest. In addition to this crucial change, various steps were made toward strengthening legal and psychiatric professional accreditation procedures and intra-professional control for quality assurance.[86] The changes include reforms of the Norwegian Board of Forensic Medicine as well as the establishment of a "National Unit for Forensic-Psychiatric Expertise." The Unit keeps an updated list of qualified forensic psychiatrists that Norwegian courts can choose from when appointing expert witnesses. The Unit acts as a guiding body in the appointment process, performs a preliminary conflict of interests check, and develops and monitors the enrolment system.[87]

5.3.2 Reforms of Compulsory Care

Another issue that became topical and politically contentious, particularly following the *Lex Breivik*, was societal protection from socially "dangerous" offenders with a legal insanity verdict.[88] Section 62 of the Penal Code was amended twice; the provision regulates the circumstances in which a

---

84 See supra Gröning (2022), C13.P17.
85 Ibid., C13.P55. See also supra Rosenqvist (2019), 76.
86 A number of requirements for the expert witnesses' qualifications and the content of their reports were introduced by FOR-2020-09-30-1921 Regulations of 30 September 2020 nr. 1921, *Regulations on Forensic Psychiatric Evaluations and Expert Witnesses*.
87 FOR-2018-02-13-240 Regulations of 13 February 2018 nr. 240, *Regulations on the Board of Forensic Medicine* and supra FOR-2020-09-30-1921. The National Unit is based at the Security-, Prison- and Forensic Psychiatry Department at St. Olavs Hospital, Trondheim.
88 P. J. Løvgren and P. T. Wiig, 'Farlige, syke personer – hjelpetrengende eller "tikkende bomber"?.' [Dangerous, sick persons: vulnerable people or "ticking bombs"?] (2022) 13 *Tidsskriftet for Den norske legeforeniging* 142.

compulsory care order can lawfully be issued by the courts for such offenders.[89] More weight is now placed on the risk of reoffending in "danger" determinations, partly shifting the focus away from the offender's criminal record:[90] when assessing "danger," the courts are to place less emphasis on "what the offender has done" and concentrate to a greater extent than before on "the more uncertain question of what the offender might do."[91] Moreover, the circumstances in which such a compulsory care order can be issued were extended. Traditionally, compulsory care is time-unlimited and presupposes that the offender has committed the most severe crimes and is a reoffending risk ("danger" requirement). Since 2016, when necessary to protect society, time-limited (up to three years) compulsory care orders can be issued for perpetrators who have committed repeated offences of a socially harmful or particularly distressing nature if the risk of reoffending is high and other measures have proved inadequate.[92] The "core target" here are "frequent offences that violate the integrity or private sphere of citizens", for example "aggravated theft."[93] These reforms seem to have led to an increase in the number of compulsory care orders issued.[94]

As Norway has no dedicated forensic-psychiatric hospitals,[95] civil and criminal psychiatry effectively compete for the same hospital beds in security-psychiatry units. In principle, the Norwegian healthcare service has discretion over the allocation of inpatient places in psychiatric wards. The decision is based on medical criteria. This principle is known as "asylum sovereignty" and it is an emanation of medical-professional authority and autonomy. At the same time, some legislative developments in the past couple of decades, including the compulsory care reforms, have given the criminal justice sector more room for ordering the hospitalisation of defendants who "do not necessarily meet traditional (medical) admission criteria."[96] Eminent figures in criminal law and forensic psychiatry have

---

89 See supra, LOV-2005-05-20-28.
90 See supra, LOV-2019-06-21-48.
91 M. Mindestrømmen, 'Impending Danger: The Meaning of Danger as a Legal Requirement for Involuntary Psychiatric Treatment in the Norwegian Criminal Justice System.' (2019) 7 *Bergen Journal of Criminal Law & Criminal Justice* 110, 117. See also supra Gröning (2023), 231–232: "To an increasing degree, compulsory psychiatric care is justified primarily by arguments that the patient poses a serious risk to others. The focus in media on serious crimes committed by mentally ill persons seems to fuel such a development".
92 LOV-2016-04-29-7 Law of 29 April 2016 nr. 7, *Act on Amendments to the 2005 Penal Code (Special Penal Reactions)*.
93 See supra Mindestrømmen (2019), 113–114.
94 See supra Gröning (2023), 231.
95 Ibid.
96 SIFER, 'Sikkerhetspsykiatri i Norge 2019' [Security psychiatry in Norway 2019]. Oslo: SIFER South-East, 2020, 23. My translation.

expressed concerns over resource scarcity – a problem that also emerged in a recent study of the impact of the reforms of Section 62 of the Penal Code that was carried out by the Norwegian National Network for Security-, Prison- and Forensic- Psychiatry (SIFER).[97] In Norway, there are approximately 4.1 security-psychiatry beds per 100,000 inhabitants, as compared to the 6.5 forensic-psychiatry beds of Sweden and the 8 of Denmark (data from 2018). In Norway, around half of these beds are occupied by criminal defendants, with the rest occupied by patients with "a danger potential that makes treatment in other wards unsafe." "There is a long waiting time for a spot," and the healthcare service may end up having to accept defendants at the expense of "perhaps even sicker patients" who have never broken the criminal law. This may compromise treatment quality for all.[98]

5.4 Conclusions: Legally Insane Offenders between Care and Societal Protection

Society's most vulnerable members deserve protection and affording that protection is a shared responsibility across all the branches of government. That is a generally accepted tenet in contemporary democracies. The legislature, the executive power, and the justice apparatus all ought to be concerned with protecting the vulnerable. A crucial issue in criminal law and justice is how to allocate that protection between offenders and victims – or *potential* victims, which alludes to societal protection. That is a difficult balance to strike for a government that is taking the rule of law seriously.

Terrorists of Breivik's calibre understandably receive little sympathy. Throughout the trial, *society* was framed as vulnerable and not the offender. The legislature went so far as introducing a so-called *Lex Breivik* aimed to provide societal protection; the case was also a key driver of

---

97 "We lack resources for this group of patients (offenders with a temporary compulsory care order) in the mental health care system", they "take spots from other severely mentally ill people", and the shortage of resources also invests follow-up care. See M. Senneseth et al (2021). 'Evaluering av konsekvensene av lovendring om særreaksjoner og varetektssur-rogat' [Assessment of the consequences of the legal change on special penal reactions and alternatives to imprisonment]. Bergen: SIFER, 22. My translation.

98 R. Rosenqvist et al, 'Helsehjelp som straffereaksjon' [Health care as a penal reaction]. Morgenbladet 12.01.2018. SIFER points out that court-ordered security-psychiatry hospitalisations "take up an increasing number of inpatient places in mental health care, at a time when the number of inpatient places available is decreasing each year". This "affects other patients who clinically have a greater treatment need" and "puts the entire mental health service, and especially security psychiatry, under pressure". See supra SIFER (2020), 23. My translation.

the subsequent insanity, forensic psychiatry and compulsory care reforms. Difficult cases do not necessarily make bad law. However, more nuanced understandings of vulnerability emerged in the public, via intra-professional (among forensic experts) and parliamentary debate, when the possible implications of new laws – beyond egregious criminal cases – became apparent. In reality, offenders with mental illness "account for a very small proportion of acts of violence in Norway"[99] and criminal reforms aimed to provide societal protection ought to take that fact into account. For offenders with mental illness, there seems to be a tension between the dimensions of care and control, depending on whether the offender is framed as a vulnerable person or a threat to others. Perhaps because the issue is so sensitive, there is conceptual confusion surrounding the relationship between these two dimensions.

An offender with a mental illness is a criminal defendant and a patient at the same time; this is frontier territory in which multiple, sometimes diverging professional logics are enforced simultaneously. Psychiatry and law may have different understandings of what it means to *be* vulnerable and to *protect* the vulnerable. They have different goals: "the goal of law is to achieve justice through conflict resolution. . . that of medicine is to restore health through consensus."[100] From this fundamental difference, several consequences stem. Medicine operates "informally and scientifically" and that does not necessarily go hand in hand with "legal procedural values" and "rules of evidence."[101] Medicine and law are strange bedfellows, which also explains the exceptional complexity of the forensic psychiatrist's role. Borrowing Gutheil's elegant phrasing, one could say that mental health professionals who "enter the realm of the expert witness. . . tread on moral terrain with a significantly different topography than the paths to which they are accustomed in their clinical roles."[102] The difference mainly invests the relationship between the professional and the subject of attention: "examiner–examinee" or "evaluator–evaluee," more than traditional doctor–patient.[103] One of the key principles in medical ethics is often expressed with the Latin phrase "*primum non nocere*," meaning "first, do not harm."[104] However, the testimony rendered by the expert witness may harm the examinee: for example, it may

99 See supra, Rosenqvist et al (2018).
100 R. Peele, P. Chodoff, 'Involuntary Hospitalization and Deinstitutionalization' in S. Bloch and S. A. Green (eds.) (2009), *Psychiatric Ethics* (4th ed.) (Oxford: OUP), 212.
101 Ibid.
102 See supra Gutheil (2009), 435.
103 Ibid., 436.
104 J. Griffiths, H. Weyers, M. Adams (eds.) *Euthanasia and Law in Europe* (Hart, Oxford, 2008), 223.

lead to punishment if the defendant is held criminally responsible.[105] Paul S. Appelbaum has suggested that for psychiatric expert witnesses, traditional principles in medical ethics, such as beneficence, are replaced by a different set of ethical standards, including truth-telling (to the patient, too) and respect for persons and justice.[106]

During and after the *Breivik* tsunami, a wave of major reforms impacted the management of offenders with mental illness in the Norwegian criminal justice system: the insanity clause was amended, forensic psychiatry was reformed along with the role of the forensic psychiatrist in insanity determinations, and the regulation of compulsory care was revised. Negotiations took place on the scope of the professional authority and autonomy of mental health professionals in the face of the criminal justice system. Different understandings of the best management of mentally ill and socially dangerous offenders emerged as "receivers of care or objects of control and incapacitation" – or both simultaneously. This tension is particularly evident today, because it has intensified under the societal-protection-oriented criminal policy pursued by the Norwegian legislature in recent years; however, it is not a new phenomenon. It is the natural effect of involving different professional logics in insanity evaluations. It is not a technical question that can be answered by using or developing new techniques of mental-state assessments, including neuroscience. It is a conceptual question and, to an extent, a sociological question that invests the dialogue between professions at both an epistemological level and at the level of social organisation. Lively intra- and inter-professional, political, and public conversations on the best management of offenders with mental illness are natural in a healthy democracy. However, during and after exceptionally hard cases with great media resonance, occasionally, these conversations take place under pressure. Perhaps that situation is not the ideal framework for a serene discussion.

Acknowledgements

The author wishes to thank Aslak Syse for reading a previous draft of this chapter.

---

105 See supra Gutheil (2009), 436. The situation is different when the psychiatrist is treating an inmate or offender in a forensic-psychiatric context; there the classic understanding of the doctor-patient relationship applies.
106 P. S. Appelbaum, 'A theory of ethics for forensic psychiatry' (1997) 25(3) *Journal of the American Academy of Psychiatry and the Law Online* 233.

6 Social Vulnerability on Trial

The Role of the Neuroscience of Trauma in Recognising Severe Social Adversity in Sentencing

Federica Coppola

6.1 Introduction

The avenues for integrating neuroscience into criminal law and justice have grown exponentially in recent years. While traditional debates have predominantly focused on the implications of neuroscientific knowledge for fundamental issues surrounding the question of criminal responsibility, such as legal insanity or the voluntariness of the criminal act, new horizons of research have expanded the scope of the potential contributions of neuroscientific evidence to broader and more nuanced aspects of criminal law and justice. For example, the relationship between punishment and social re-integration, the legitimacy of harsh prison conditions, and the prevention of state abuses against private citizens (at risk of being) in conflict with the justice system.[1]

With specific regard to the so-called 'vulnerable' defendants on trial, scholarly discussions about the applications of neuroscientific evidence are gradually moving from controversial uses of "brain-based syndromes" in the ambit of criminal defences to more far-reaching justice issues, including the impact of adverse socio-contextual factors on the brain and behaviour, and their relevance for the criminal process. In contrast with the individualistic approaches to crime that still pervade criminal law, these discussions have begun to highlight the potential contributions of neuroscience by addressing the close relationship between social injustice and criminal justice. Indeed, several commentators call for more substantive contributions from neuroscience research to identify avenues

---

1 See eg S. Lightart et al., 'Prison and the Brain: Neuropsychological Research in the Light of the European Convention of Human Rights' (2019) 10 *NJECL* 187; F. Coppola, 'The Brain in Solitude: An(other) Eighth Amendment Challenge to Solitary Confinement (2019) 7 *JLB* 184; H. Teshone, 'The Neural Underlings of Unconscious Racial Biases and Its Effect on Police Behavior' (*CSN*, April 2019) <https://neuroethics.upenn.edu/wp-content/uploads/2019/08/TESHOME_CNS-Final-.pdf> accessed 10 December 2022.

DOI: 10.4324/9781003331056-7

for addressing social, economic, and racial inequalities in criminal justice matters.[2]

This chapter takes up these recent strands of scholarship to discuss the use of the neuroscience of trauma to address severe social vulnerability in criminal trials, focusing on the U.S. criminal legal system. For the purpose of the chapter, severe social vulnerability includes a person's chronic or repeated exposure to severe social adversity, such as extreme socio-economic deprivation, personal and institutional abuse and neglect, exposure to personal and community violence, and severe discrimination. Although neuroscience alone can hardly assess the impact of such social determinants of crime in the context of criminal trials, the chapter argues that neuroscience can indirectly do so by offering additional evidence of the traumatic effects of these forms of severe social adversity in cases by evidencing a link between such adversity and the crime committed. Notably, the chapter suggests that mitigation claims should be allowed to (also) include *individualised* or *framework;*[3] evidence of the neurobiological and neuropsychological effects of trauma from severe social adversity to reinforce the link between the defendant's conduct and the adversities endured. Hence, the chapter uses neuroscience to support the application of sentencing schemes that recognise severe social adversity as a mitigating factor and acknowledge, albeit implicitly, the structural problematics that often participate in the genesis of offending.

The chapter is structured as follows: section 6.2 canvasses state-of-the-art behavioural and neuroscientific literature about the effects of trauma from severe social adversity. Section 6.3 reviews the current consideration of severe social adversity in the death penalty and youth sentencing, including the contribution of neuroscientific evidence of trauma from such adversity to mitigation claims in these contexts. Section 6.4 argues for expanding the mitigating relevance of severe social adversity to adult noncapital sentencing and discusses avenues for integrating neuroscientific evidence in legal representation. Section 6.5 concludes the chapter with forward-looking remarks about permitting (neuro)scientific evidence of trauma from severe social adversity in sentencing hearings. The section proposes that a sentencing system sensitive to defendants' traumatic backgrounds is critical for identifying responses that address the individual and social needs of this class of vulnerable defendants, providing such defendants with constructive opportunities for healing and rehabilitation, and promoting fairness and equality.

---

2 See e.g., O. Rollins, *Conviction: The Making and Unmaking of the Violent Brain* (Stanford University Press 2021).

3 See F. Coppola, 'When the Brain Can Make a Difference: Individualized vs. Framework Uses of Neuroscience in Courtroom' (2020) 1 *DPU* 1.

6.2 The Trauma of Severe Social Adversity

Trauma is endemic in criminal justice settings, with some studies[4] finding that over 90 per cent of incarcerated people have experienced trauma in their lifetime. Although the sources of trauma are varied, much of the trauma that affects people who come into contact with the criminal legal system originates in severe social adversity. Indeed, empirical research shows that many system-impacted people have survived social deprivation, personal abuse, institutional neglect, or structural racism.[5] In many cases, the traumatic nature of these experiences, especially when repeated or chronic, plays a determining role in the genesis of offending.

Before analysing the traumatic effects of severe social adversity, an important terminological clarification is warranted: What is trauma? Answering this question is all but obvious, as one of the challenges in talking about "trauma" is that this term lacks a consistent definition in the literature. Under one (and more intuitive) approach, trauma is narrowly defined as one's experience of a shocking and emotionally overwhelming event, such as an earthquake or an act of terrorism.[6] By partial contrast, a broader and more largely supported account qualifies trauma as an individual's response to a deeply distressful, disturbing, or shocking event – or a combination of such negative events – implying immediate and long-term adverse psychological and behavioural effects.[7] So comprehensively framed, trauma is the *imprint*[8] of overwhelming events experienced as physically or emotionally harmful, with tangible effects on the individual's physical, social, and emotional functioning and well-being.[9]

4 See e.g., L. J. Jäggi et al., 'The Relationship between Trauma, Arrest, and Incarceration History among Black Americans: Findings from the National Survey of American Life' (2016) 6 *SMH* 187.

5 E.g., M. T. Berg and R. Loeber, 'Examining the Neighborhood Context of the Violent Offending-victimization Relationship: A Prospective Investigation' (2011) 27 *JQC* 427; W. G. Jennings et al., 'On the Overlap between Victimization and Offending: A Review of the Literature' (2012) 17 *Aggression and Violent Behavior* 16; C. Haney, *Criminality in Context: The Psychological Foundations of Criminal Justice* (APA 2020).

6 Substance Abuse and Mental Health Service Administration (SAMHSA), *Trauma and Violence*, < https://www.samhsa.gov/trauma-violence> (accessed 3 December 2022).

7 See S. F. Cole et al., 'Mass Advocates for Children, Helping Traumatized Children Learn: Supportive School Environments for Children Traumatized by Family Violence' (2005) < https://traumasensitiveschools.org/wp-content/uploads/2013/06/Helping-Traumatized-Children-Learn.pdf> (accessed 3 December 2022) ("Experts explain that trauma is not an event itself, but rather a response to a stressful experience in which a person's ability to cope is dramatically undermined").

8 See B. Van Der Kolk, *The Body Keeps the Score: Brain, Mind, and Body in the Healing of Trauma* (Penguin Books 2014) 21.

9 *Id.*

Under this approach, trauma encompasses both objective and subjective components.[10] The objective component (also known as "event," "source," or "stressor")[11] includes the occurrence of or one's exposure to a shocking, deeply distressing, or disturbing experience. Such experience may consist of one or multiple events,[12] or prolonged or chronic exposure to situations perceived or experienced as traumatic. When serious adversity is the source of trauma, the types of events or situations that can be perceived or experienced as traumatic are both personal and structural, or a combination of them.[13] The most typical adversity-related personal events include severe, repeated, or chronic abuse (physical, emotional, sexual), direct exposure to violence, abandonment, and/or neglect. On the other hand, the structural sources of trauma may include a variety of social harms, such as extreme social deprivation, status-based discrimination, persistent inequality, institutional neglect, and "biographic racism."[14]

Regardless of its source, trauma relates to the individual's subjective *experience* of it;[15] people can experience a traumatic event in various ways. Much of this variety depends on different variables, such as a person's demographics (age, gender, etc.) or cultural background. On average, traumatic events are experienced by an individual as physically or emotionally harmful or threatening. Experiencing trauma can "overwhelm the individual's ability to cope and elicit intense feelings such as fear, terror, helplessness, hopelessness, and despair."[16]

Furthermore, trauma entails *effects*.[17] Such effects may either materialise in the aftermath of the event and wane after a short time, or they can grow and manifest over time and persist accordingly. Typical effects of traumatic exposures include, but are not limited to, emotional numbness, dissociation, chronic anxiety, hypervigilance, hyperresponsivity to a perceived threat, heightened rejection sensitivity, self-isolation, alienation,

---

10 See G. Griffin and S. Sallen, 'Considering Child Trauma Issues in Juvenile Court Sentencing' (2013) 34 *Child Legal RTS. J.* 1, 6–8.

11 See *id.,* 6.

12 Prolonged exposures to or victimization by multiple traumatic events such as violence and abuse, coupled with severe environmental deprivation associated with endemic poverty, are labelled as *complex trauma*s. See e.g., J. Briere and C. Scott, 'Complex Trauma in Adolescents and Adults: Effects and Treatment' (2015) 38 *PCNA* 515.

13 For instance, economically deprived children are more likely to experience personal traumas such as violence and sexual abuse. See e.g., D. Dante Troutt, 'Trapped in Tragedies, Spatial Inequality and Law' (2018) 101 *MULR* 603, 612.

14 See Haney, *supra* note 5.

15 Griffin and Sallen, *supra* note 10, 6.

16 *Id.,* 7.

17 *Id.,* 8.

and overwhelming social fears.[18] In most extreme cases, individuals may develop mental health issues such as post-traumatic stress disorder (PTSD),[19] psychosis, or schizophrenia, as well as alcohol and substance abuse disorders. Behaviourally, trauma can result in behaviours that harm the sufferer and others; such harmful behaviours are sometimes associated with criminal conduct.[20]

The psychological and behavioural effects of trauma, including severe social adversity, reflect alterations occurring in the brain. A vast array of research has indicated that trauma fundamentally changes neurobiology and causes psychological symptoms and social maladaptation – often throughout one's life. From a neurobiological standpoint, overwhelming adversity causes *stress* that exceeds one's ability to cope with it.[21] This type of stress is labelled as *toxic stress*.[22] Toxic stress entails the repeated or prolonged activation of the biological stress response system. When toxic stress response occurs continually – that is, when the biological stress system is frequently heightened due to prolonged adversity – it can affect brain pathways like the hippocampus, the amygdala, and various regions of the prefrontal cortex,[23] which govern psychological functions such as self-regulation, perception, responsivity to social cues, impulse control, and emotion regulation. These alterations can impact psychological functioning in ways that can cumulatively be damaging to long-term physical and mental health. These psychological alterations have been associated with a heightened risk of maladaptive tendencies and behaviours, including hostility, rule-breaking, aggression, and violence.[24]

Importantly, not everybody exposed to trauma undergoes the same effects to the same extent because the experience of trauma is highly

---

18 B. Van Der Kolk, *supra* note 8, 170.

19 See eg M. Gohara, 'In Defense of the Injured: How Trauma-Informed Criminal Defense Can Reform Sentencing' (2018) 45 *AJCLR* 1, 15 (correctly emphasising that "the effects of trauma are by no means limited to PTSD. Exclusive focus on this diagnosis risks missing other profound effects of trauma on people whose symptoms, though detrimental, may fall short of the disorder's clinical definition").

20 E.g., J. Garbarino, 'Foreword: Pathways from Childhood Trauma to Adolescent Violence and Delinquency' (2002) 6 *JAMT* xxv; A. N. Schore, 'Early Relational Trauma, Disorganized Attachment, and the Development of a Predisposition to Violence' in D. Siegel and M. Solomon (eds), *Healing trauma: Attachment, Mind, Body, and Brain* (WW Norton & Company 2003).

21 J. D. Bremner, 'Traumatic Stress: Effects on the Brain' (2006) 8 *Dialogues in Clinical Neuroscience* 445.

22 H. Franke, 'Toxic Stress: Effects, Prevention Treatment' (2014) 1 *Children* 390; Sonja Lupien et al., 'Effects of Stress throughout the Lifespan on the Brain, Behavior and Cognition' (2009) 10 *Nature Reviews* 434.

23 See Bremner, *supra* note 21.

24 For a review, see F. Coppola, *The Emotional Brain and the Guilty Mind: Novel Paradigms of Culpability and Punishment* (Hart Publishing 2021).

subjective; individuals exposed to the same potentially traumatic experiences may endure differing reactions. Subjective reactions to trauma depend on a variety of factors, such as one's age, resilience, coping strategies, the duration of the traumatic event, and, more fundamentally, the presence of so-called *buffers* (or protective factors) like proper treatment or social and emotional support, which can mediate the effects of trauma on the individual. Usually, when trauma exposures are prolonged and *unbuffered*, their impact on an individual's well-being, health, and social functioning may be long-lasting or even permanent.

The correlation between trauma from severe social adversity and problematic life trajectories, including the engagement in harmful conduct like criminal behaviour, is "today accept[ed] as axiomatic"[25] in the literature. While causal chains are admittedly complex, a consensus exists that chronic or acute exposure to various forms of severe social adversity may carry – among other implications – criminogenic effects.

For instance, in his compelling work on the contextualisation of crime,[26] psychologist Craig Haney has eloquently illustrated the harmful and criminogenic effects (both direct and indirect) of structural factors such as racism, early institutionalisation, and poverty, including their links to personal traumas such as maltreatment and abuse. While reporting on the criminogenic effects of these forms of adversity via trauma mechanisms, Haney has pointed out the relationship between aggregate levels of *situational stress* and criminal conduct. As he has put it, the accumulation or chronicity of adverse social conditions can be so "psychologically painful and can have a number of long-term negative consequences"[27] that mental health professionals regard these effects as a type of "traumatic stress. . . that can undermine behavioral adjustment in a wide range of settings" and "lead to an increased likelihood of delinquent and criminal behavior."[28]

For Haney, even the continued presence in criminogenic situations can lead to persistence in law-breaking, often as a means of survival. So framed, criminogenic contexts constitute situational opportunities and demands for law-breaking conduct and barriers to desistance. In some criminogenic contexts, criminal offending becomes a way to adapt to and survive such contexts, especially when institutional support is lacking or unhelpful. That is, criminal behaviour becomes a form of adaptation – a coping mechanism to adjust to the pathological demands of traumatising contexts and situations.

---

25 Gohara, *supra* note 19, 19.
26 Haney, *supra* note 5.
27 *Id.*
28 *Id.*

Neuroscientific insights are consistent with behavioural data. Although studies explicitly addressing the links between social adversity and crime via neurobiological mechanisms are still scant,[29] the available research adds an important layer of evidence about the links between adverse social contexts and unhealthy behavioural outcomes via neurobiological alterations. For instance, some research[30] has explored the relationship between cortisol levels (i.e., biological stress response), toxic environmental stressors, and violence, especially in adolescence and young adulthood. Taken together, these studies have associated exposure to violence and contextual stressors with elevated cortisol levels, hypervigilance, and hyperresponsivity to threats in the long term. Chronic or long-lasting hyper-responsivity to threats also explains why people (especially youth) who live in disadvantaged communities may become more vulnerable to aggressive reactions or even experience "pathological adaptations," including desensitisation to violence.[31] These factors have been associated with problematic decision-making under risk conditions[32] and a higher risk of engaging in maladaptive behaviours. Importantly, these findings align with behavioural studies on gang-involved youth,[33] indicating higher percentages of PTSD and other trauma-related symptoms compared to other youth. As these studies have suggested,[34] in underserved, violent, and overpoliced neighbourhoods, gang affiliation becomes a means for protection, safety, and belonging, as well as an outlet for ostracism – especially for early trauma sufferers.

Altogether, the available insights into the neurobiological impacts of trauma offer important complementary evidence to draw links between exposures to damaged backgrounds and crime via the neurobiological mechanisms of trauma. As noticed above, enduring traumatic stress can precipitate adverse structural and functional changes to the brain that risk

---

29 See generally Rollins, *supra* note 3.
30 See e.g., S. Aiyer et al, 'Exposure to Violence Predicting Cortisol Response During Adolescence and Early Adulthood: Understanding Moderating Factors' (2014) 43 *JYA* 1066.
31 See J. Garbarino et al., 'Mitigating the Effects of Gun Violence on Children and Youth' (2002) 12 *The Future of Children* 73.
32 E.g., A. J. Porcelli and MR Delgado 'Acute Stress Modulates Risk Taking in Financial Decision-making' (2009) 20 *Psychological Science* 278; K. Starcke et al., 'Anticipatory Stress Influences Decision Making under Explicit Risk Conditions' (2008) 122 *Behavioral Neuroscience* 1352.
33 See National Child Traumatic Stress Network, 'Trauma in the Lives of Gang-involved Youth: Tips for Volunteers and Community Organizations' (2009) 2; N. Adams et al., 'The Relationship Between Childhood Traumatic Experiences and Gang-Involved Delinquent Behavior in Adolescent Boys' (2009) *JACSEP* 6.
34 Adams et al., *id.; see also* Samantha Buckingham, 'Trauma-Informed Juvenile Justice', 53 *AJCLR* 641, 658.

altering psychological health and social functioning, including a higher risk of engaging in harmful behaviour like criminal conduct. More indirectly, this body of knowledge can add an important layer of evidence for bringing disadvantaged backgrounds to the fore of the criminal process and supporting justice mechanisms that mitigate, rather than exacerbate, the detrimental effects of severe social adversity.

6.3 *De Iure Condito*: Severe Social Adversity through the Neuroscience of Trauma in Capital and Youth Sentencing

In principle, evidence of severe trauma may be a factor for sentencing mitigation. Notwithstanding, and despite the overrepresentation of traumatised defendants in criminal trials, there is no consistent approach to how sentencing systems treat trauma in the U.S. On average, people with serious histories of trauma from severe social adversity rarely obtain a penalty discount in the federal system.[35] On the other hand, some states[36] are more prone to confer sentencing discounts to traumatised defendants; however, case law analyses have suggested that courts rarely afford a mitigating weight to traumas – no matter how severe they are – but tend to privilege other sentencing goals, notably public safety.

The domains in which trauma from severe social adversity has received more prominence include cases involving the adult death penalty and youth life sentencing. The constitutional and procedural reasons for such "special" treatment are manifold and doctrinally traceable to the principle that both capital and young defendants are "constitutionally different"[37] from other defendant populations. Because "death is different," capital defendants are entitled to a constitutional right to present any form of mitigating evidence, including about their damaged backgrounds,[38]

---

35 For a federal case law analysis, see Gohara, *supra* note 19, 25-32.
36 E.g., New York State. See also M. Bagaric et al, 'Trauma and Sentencing: The Case for Mitigating Penalty for Childhood Physical and Sexual Abuse' (2019) 30 *SLPR* 1.
37 *Ford v Wainwright* 477 U.S. 399 (1986); *Harmelin v Michigan* 501 U.S. 957 (1991); *Roper v Simmons* 543 U.S. 551, 569-570 (2005); *Graham v Florida* 560 U.S. 48, 68 (2010); *Miller v Alabama* 567 U.S. 460, 132 S. Ct. 2455, 2465 (2012); *Montgomery v Louisiana* 136 S. Ct. 718, 736 (2016).
38 E.g., *Penry v Lynaugh* 492 U.S. 302, 319 (1989), *abrogated on other grounds* ("[E]vidence about [a] defendant's background and character is relevant" to the sentencing decision, "because of the belief, long held by this society, that defendants who commit criminal acts that are attributable to a disadvantaged background, or to emotional and mental problems, may be less culpable than defendants who have no such excuse").

to avoid the "ultimate penalty."[39] Accordingly, defence attorneys are constitutionally obliged to investigate their clients' backgrounds, and juries must weigh the evidence of adversity during their deliberations if presented.[40]

Youth facing life sentences do not enjoy the same constitutional right as capital defendants. However, following the Supreme Court's recognition that children who offend cannot be treated as adults in view of their young age, an investigation into their background is factually required – albeit it is not constitutionally mandatory.[41] As children who offend are still psychologically and neurologically developing, evidence of disadvantaged backgrounds is considered to be key in demonstrating their particular vulnerabilities and, thus, supporting their diminished culpability at the time of their crimes that can warrant less harsh penalties.

It is important to emphasise that neuroscience has recently played more of a central role in sentencing contexts. For youth sentencing, the famous landmark cases of *Graham*,[42] *Miller*,[43] and *Montgomery*[44] have demonstrated the preponderant role of neuroscientific knowledge in supporting arguments for sentencing that children should not be treated the same way as adults due to their psycho-social immaturity at the time of their offences. A key neuroscientific contribution included insights into children's particular vulnerability to socio-environmental influences in view of their ongoing neurodevelopment. These insights were fundamental to supporting the argument that children are particularly vulnerable to the harmful and criminogenic effects of damaged contexts precisely because of their underdeveloped capacities for judgment, control, and resilience. Even more importantly, these insights prompted the Court (especially in *Miller*) to include the defendants' backgrounds as an additional criterion for assessing their diminished culpability.

For the death penalty, neuroscientific evidence of trauma has often led juries to give weight to severe social adversity and reduce a sentence from death to life imprisonment. For example, in an in-depth study[45] on the current uses of neuroscience research on childhood trauma[46] in

---

39 *Gregg v Georgia* 428 U.S. 153 (1976); *Woodson v Carolina* 428 U.S. 280, 303-5 (1976); *Lockett v Ohio* 438 U.S. 586, 608 (1978).
40 See e.g., *Wiggins v Smith* 539 U.S. 510 (2003); *Rompilla v Beard* 545 U.S. 374 (2005). See also P. L. Crocker, 'Childhood Abuse and Adult Murder: Implications for the Death Penalty' (1999) 77 *North Caroline L. Rev.* 1143.
41 See *Jones v Mississippi* 593 U.S. (2021).
42 *Graham v Florida* 560 U.S. 48, 68 (2010).
43 *Miller v Alabama* 567 U.S. 460, 132 S. Ct. 2455 (2012).
44 *Montgomery v Louisiana* 136 S. Ct. 718 (2016).
45 See D. Denno, 'How Courts in Criminal Cases Respond to Childhood Trauma' (2019) 103 *Marquette LR* 301.
46 See *id.*, 314, fn. 62

capital cases, Deborah Denno has illustrated the persuasive role of neuroscientific evidence for claims of mitigation and ineffective assistance of counsel. Importantly, Denno's study has indicated that courts tend to admit many different types of neuroscientific tests to support a variety of trauma-related conditions, ranging from neurological disorders to brain damage to psychiatric diagnoses. As she has emphasised, although "evidence of brain damage [from childhood trauma] may not be sufficient [. . .], it does enable courts to better perceive childhood trauma as mitigating if they accept its validity."[47]

Aside from cases involving more extreme punishments, traumas from serious adversity such as a history of abuse and neglect are more rarely and inconsistently considered in noncapital cases..[48] Also, adversities that arise from unchecked social harms such as extreme socio-economic deprivation, racism, or abusive institutionalisation are even less regarded[49] in mitigation claims – regardless of their salience to the relevant case.

The inconsistency that characterises the relevance of evidence of trauma from severe social adversity in noncapital cases has several rationales. Foremost, there is no constitutional obligation to introduce and evaluate evidence of damaged backgrounds in noncapital cases, even when defendants may face life sentences without parole. Further, this lack of provision has resulted in defence attorneys often failing to properly investigate their clients' social history and incorporate such history in their arguments for sentencing leniency.[50] It has also led the courts to discount traumatic adversity and to commonly refuse downward departures because most defendants have suffered adversity in their lives. Notably, "the ubiquity of disadvantage in defendant's lives provides little basis for differentiation among them" to find extraordinary mitigating circumstances.[51]

---

47 *Id.,* 322.

48 See Bagaric et al., *supra* note 36, 12–23 (analysing the inconsistent approach to childhood trauma in four state sentencing systems including California, Texas, New York and Florida and evidencing that no statutory provisions in these jurisdictions embody such mitigating factors).

49 See Gohara, *supra* note 19, 26. See also M. Bagaric, 'Rich Offender, Poor Offender: Why It (Sometimes) Matter in Sentencing' (2015) 33 *Minnesota Journal of Law & Inequality* 1, 19-21.

50 See M. Gohara, 'Grace Notes: A Case for Making Mitigation the Heart of Noncapital Sentencing', 41 *AMJCRL* 41, 59 (emphasising "the significant gulf between the noncapital guidelines' recommendations for essential sentencing advocacy and prevailing defense practice in many jurisdictions, especially those strapped for resources.").

51 Gohara, *supra* note 19, 27.

Relatedly, the disregard for traumas from severe social adversity also originates in the pervasive biases[52] towards structural sources of trauma, which may lead the courts to view the defendants' traumas as less 'credible' and less 'serious' than the traumas that follow from other types of stressors such as war combat.[53] This is all the more true if one considers that sentencing evaluations are often influenced by – and therefore express – the sentencer's emotional attitudes towards the person on trial, including characteristics such as the person's social background, education, employment, or race; tellingly, numerous empirical studies[54] have indicated that courts tend to impose harsher sentences on less educated, poor, and unemployed people, as well as on those belonging to minority groups.

Ultimately, the magnitude of implicit biases towards defendants with damaged backgrounds is fueled by insufficient knowledge of and training on trauma and its effects on legal actors, including judges, prosecutors, and attorneys. On the one hand, poor education about trauma from severe social adversity, including its close relationships to offending, can lead legal actors to fail to inquire into the defendants' social history. On the other hand, and even more concerningly, trauma symptoms are frequently misinterpreted as aggressive or lacking in empathy or labelled as antisocial personality disorder – all conditions that may be taken as aggravating evidence and used to support harsher sentences.[55]

Against this backdrop, and considering the breadth and pervasiveness of unresolved trauma from severe social adversity among convicted people, the normalisation of routinised trauma-informed sentencing practices is a pressing procedural issue. This issue also involves a discussion on the contribution of the neuroscience of trauma in bringing severe social adversity to the fore of criminal trials.

---

52 See B. Donald and E. Bakies, 'A Glimpse Inside the Brain's Black Box: Understanding the Role of Neuroscience in Criminal Sentencing' (2016) 85 *Fordham LR* 482, 499–500.

53 See *id.* See also B. Grey, 'Neuroscience, PTSD, and Sentencing Mitigation' (2012) 34 *Cardozo LR* 93 (observing that "legal systems identify certain stressors in particular environments that justify leniency within the criminal justice system, while denying leniency to other stressors, without fully explaining why" – as if some stressors were more privileged than others).

54 See e.g., C. Betsey, 'Income and Wealth Transfer Effects of Discrimination in Sentencing' (2005) 32 *The Review of Black Political Economy* 111; The Sentencing Project, Racial Disparity in Sentencing (January 2005) https://www.opensocietyfoundations.org/publications/racial-disparity-sentencing accessed 12 December 2022; Frank Baumgartner et al., 'Racial Resentment and the Death Penalty' (2022) *JREP* 1.

55 See Buckingham, *supra* note 34, 656; Gohara *supra* note 19, 22 (both highlighting this problematic aspect).

6.4　*De Iure Condendo*: Making the Case for Social Vulnerability in Noncapital Adult Sentencing (Also) through the Neuroscience of Trauma

The irrelevance of severe social adversity to sentencing mitigation in noncapital cases has become largely indefensible. Limiting the relevance of such adversity to capital and youth life sentencing lacks both factual and normative grounds, as the quality and extent of traumas stemming from serious adversity suffered by different kinds of defendants are likely comparable.[56] Moreover, even though consideration of a defendant's damaged background is not constitutionally required, courts enjoy broad discretion at sentencing to better consider vast amounts of information about the defendants, including information about defendants' damaged backgrounds, to calibrate their sentencing determinations.[57]

From a substantive standpoint, the mitigating relevance of the trauma from severe social adversity finds its rationale in the defendant's diminished culpability at the time of the crime. Criminal acts that occur in the context of traumatic adversity should warrant sentencing leniency insofar as such adversity is proved to compellingly diminish the defendant's ability to conform their behaviour to the law by either impacting their mental capacity or limiting their opportunity to do otherwise. If a person's opportunities and options to conform their behaviour to the law are limited by their exposure to serious adversity – which they did not choose and over which they had little or no control – then such adversity may gain practical and normative significance in terms of diminished culpability and blameworthiness.

Foremost, neuroscientific and behavioural literature suggests that traumas from severe social adversity can damage the very cognitive, emotional, and volitional domains that are centrally relevant to a person's blameworthiness,[58] such as the capacity for self-control, judgment, and empathetic responding. Tellingly, such damages do not vanish when a person reaches the age of 18, but they can arise, manifest, and grow at later stages of life and endure over time. Thus, a plausible normative argument for the mitigating value of such trauma focuses on its bearing on the defendant's mental capacity at the time of the crime.[59]

From a related but not mutually exclusive perspective, the mitigating force of trauma from severe social adversity lies in the choice-limiting

---

56　See also Gohara, *id.*, 26.
57　See *United States v Booker* 543 U.S. 220 (2005) (stating that Federal Sentencing Guidelines are advisory only).
58　See generally Coppola, *supra* note 5.
59　See also N. Lacey, 'Socializing the Subject of Criminal Law? Criminal Responsibility and the Purposes of Criminalization' (2016) 99 *MLR* 541.

effects of such adversity.[60] This argument shifts the focus of the mitigation from the "pathology" of the person (the *effects* of trauma) to the pathology of the socio-contextual factors (the *source* of trauma) that may have influenced the criminal choice. Specifically, the argument goes that unbuffered, lifetime adversities constitute *objective situational pressures* that place individuals in circumstances of authentically hard choices, even if their rational mental capacities remain substantially uncompromised. From this perspective, people facing severe social hardships must be considered rational actors. However, they constantly face choices that need to adapt or respond to pathological situations and social environments in which choice is limited and motivation to engage with the law is reduced. For these normative reasons, people have a diminished, fair opportunity to do otherwise and, therefore, should be less culpable for criminal offences in cases in which choices are limited by situational pressures, such as living in extreme deprivation or having to survive community violence.

Procedurally, traumas from severe social adversity can gather their space in noncapital hearings within existing sentencing regimes via a thorough investigation into the defendant's background to persuade the courts to better "visualise" the defendant's trauma and apprehend its salience to the relevant offence. As previously suggested, when defence attorneys gather knowledge of their client's exposure to a given source of trauma, that exploration should carefully delve into the effects of such a source on the defendant's behaviour to allow sentencers to "view defendants' actions *in [the] context of their own victimization.*"[61] This requires that defence teams adequately represent the individualised presence and relevance of trauma to the defendant's diminished culpability and argue for sentencing leniency.[62] Ideally, such exploration and representation should include not only significant traumas that have a direct link with the offence (that is, traumas that are the principal reason for its commission) but also those that contributed to it.[63]

Thus, a sound use of neuroscience may be key in this context. Exposing the courts to empirical evidence on trauma is fundamental for presenting a robust and persuasive account of how tangibly and empirically severe social adversity can impact a defendant's behavioural domains

---

60 See Coppola, *supra* note 5, 196.
61 Gohara, *supra* note 19, 8 (my emphasis).
62 See also generally Gohara, *supra* note 19.
63 See eg *United States v Matney*, 375 F. Supp. 2d 482, 488 (W.D. Va. 2005) (recognising that diminished capacity need not be the sole cause of the offence to justify a departure, but should "comprise. . . a *contributing* factor in the commission of the offense") (citation omitted). See also *Miller v Alabama*, *supra* note 43 (introducing the defendant's "pathological background" as the contributing reason behind his commission of the crime).

relevant for culpability. To be sure, neuroscience cannot demonstrate a nexus between trauma and the commission of an offence, and it is unlikely it will ever be able to do so. Nevertheless, depending on the relevant case, neuroscience could be an effective tool to validate adversity-based mitigation claims insofar as it provides supplemental information about how a defendant's traumatic exposure to severe social adversity may have affected their behaviour in a way that is relevant for culpability. When conditions exist, neuroscience can be introduced as *individualised evidence*[64] to support trauma-related conditions linked to the defendant's exposure to social adversity. When individualised assessments are not an option, defence attorneys should still be able to introduce neuroscience as *framework evidence*[65] to instruct the courts about the generalised neurobiological effects of trauma from social adversity and possibly use that evidence to corroborate psychological assessments. For instance, courts can be instructed about the stress-induced changes to the brain following trauma and how such changes can explain the psychological and behavioural outcomes for a relevant defendant.

Proper use of research on the neuroscience of trauma presupposes solid knowledge of it on the part of defence attorneys. To this end, attorneys should be equipped with adequate scientific training about the effects of trauma to present evidence of severe social adversity in a way that is empirically sound, normatively relevant, and accessible to the court. As increasing numbers of studies show links between severe social adversity and criminal offences via the detrimental mechanisms of trauma, it is imperative that legal actors fully appreciate these links and properly engage with scientific evidence to develop solid mitigation claims. The introduction of trauma evidence is a crucial aspect of legally representing socially vulnerable defendants. Most importantly, it is key to afford such defendants better informed, more proportionate, and safer sentencing options and to do them better justice.

6.5 Trauma-Informed Sentencing to Recognise Social Vulnerability and Do Better Justice

To conclude this chapter, it is worth offering a few final remarks on *why* noncapital sentencing hearings should normally permit (neuro)scientific evidence of trauma from social adversity. As emphasised in the previous section, such evidence may be critical for validating mitigation claims and lead to sentences more proportionate to a defendant's actual culpability,

---

64 See Coppola *supra* note 3.
65 *Id.*

given their disadvantaged backgrounds. Nevertheless, a sentencing reduction is not the only justice outcome that a trauma-informed sentencing system can and should aspire to.

From a broader and more forward-looking perspective, the acknowledgement of serious adversity through the lenses of the (neuro)science of trauma can critically lead sentencing authorities to overcome implicit biases towards defendants of disadvantaged groups; further, it can help to foster sentencing options that properly address such defendants' individual and social needs, offer better transformational opportunities, and promote pathways of healing and rehabilitation.[66] That is, a recognition of severe social adversity should receive a quantitative (mitigating) weight and, more importantly, be valued as a qualitative benchmark for determining the most appropriate options when responding to offences and addressing defendants' problematic backgrounds and needs. Admittedly, a proper apprehension of the impacts of severe social adversity on the defendants' life trajectories could incentivise sentencing authorities to identify alternative sentencing options that a while addressing the crime, also seek to minimise the risk of re-traumatisation.[67]

Philosophically, introducing the (neuro)science of trauma in cases of defendants with damaged backgrounds can be crucial to mitigating the many social injustices at the root of many criminal behaviours. Indeed, acknowledging and affording weight to trauma from social adversity in sentencing entails an implicit recognition of the state's role in contributing to, or failing to resolve, the structural factors that facilitated trauma exposures. This claim is consistent with recent voices[68] in the literature that argue for the introduction of sentencing schemes that explicitly acknowledge state contributions to the production of social harms that induced the defendant to commit the crime, including the recognition of state responsibility in structuring the inequalities that either precipitated or perpetuated criminogenic conditions – especially to the damage of most disadvantaged groups.

The criminal legal system can play a key role in preventing and resolving, instead of reproducing, trauma from social adversity. Accordingly, the criminal legal system must be fully equipped to grasp the complex and consistent relationships between social adversity and crime by working

---

66 See also Gohara, *supra* note 50, 69 (suggesting that sentencing should place an "emphasis on positive factors in the defendant's life, such as educational and employment opportunities, family support, and access to and amenability to rehabilitative services").

67 K. Thomas, 'Beyond Mitigation: Towards a Theory of Allocution' (2007) 75 *Fordham L. Rev.* 2641, 2645.

68 Eg M. Manikis, 'Recognising State Blame in Sentencing: A Communicative and Relational Framework' (2022) 81 *The Cambridge Law Journal* 294.

towards maximising endeavours that respond to traumatised socially vulnerable defendants in ways that address both the harms they suffered and those inflicted on victims and communities. Science, in general, and neuroscience can be a potent tool to enable criminal justice to achieve this goal.

6.6 Conclusion

Trauma from social adversity is an overrepresented phenomenon in the U.S. criminal legal system. Despite increasing awareness of the harms and injustice of such overrepresentation, the criminal legal system largely continues to turn a blind eye to defendants with traumatic backgrounds. Notably, it perpetuates counterproductive patterns of sentencing and punishment that reproduce the mechanisms of such trauma instead of interrupting them.

The word "trauma" comes from the ancient Greek τραῦμα, for "wound". Neuroscience can make such a wound visible and enable the criminal legal system to heal it instead of making it even more profound. Ensuring that the justice system can visualise this pervasive wound and take innovative action for change and reform is imperative. Most fundamentally, such an action requires an enormous interdisciplinary educational effort on the part of legal actors. As enormous as it is, this effort is just the barest step to addressing the injustices suffered by the many socially vulnerable defendants that populate the U.S. criminal legal system.

Bibliography

A. Bechara, 'Emotion, Decision Making and the Orbitofrontal Cortex' (2000) 10 *Cerebral Cortex* 295–307.

A. Corda and R. Hester, 'Leaving the Shining City on a Hill: A Plea for Rediscovering Comparative Criminal Justice Policy in the United States' (2021) 31(2) *International Criminal Justice Review* 203–223

A. Dafnos, 'Lone Wolf Terrorism as Category: Learning from the Breivik Case' (2013) 3 *Journal Exit-Deutschland. Zeitschrift für Deradikalisierung und Demokratische Kultur* 96–114

A. Giordano, 'Intelligenza Artificiale e Giusto Processo Civile' (2022) *L'intelligenza artificiale tra scienza, etica e diritto* (Munera).

A. Kirkevik, 'Breivik-paragrafane – Kollektiv staff for psykisk sjuke' [The Breivik Law – Collective Punishment for the Mentally Ill] (2012) 2 *Syn og Segn*.

A. Løvlie, 'Criminal Insanity: Concepts and Evidence' (2019) 7 *Bergen Journal of Criminal Law & Criminal Justice* 78–96.

A. Owusu-Bempah, 'The Interpretation and Application of the Right to Effective Participation' (2018) 22(4) *International Journal of Evidence & Proof* 321–341

A. Ross, *On Law and Justice* (Stevens & Sons 1958).

A. Syse, 'Breivik–the Norwegian Terrorist Case' (2014) 32 *Behavioral Sciences & the Law* 389–401.

A. Syse, 'Tvungent psykisk helsevern' [Compulsory Care] (2016) 42 *Kritisk juss* 278.

A. Wertheimer, *Coercion* (Princeton University Press 1987).

A. Wertheimer and F. G. Miller, 'There are (STILL) No Coercive Offers' (2014) 40 *Journal of Medical Ethics* 392–393.

American Psychiatric Association, *Diagnostic and Statistical Manual of Mental Disorders* (5th edn, American Psychiatric Association, Text Revision 2022).

B. Brody and J. Engelhardt (eds), *Mental Illness: Law and Public Policy, Philosophy and Medicine* (D. Reidel 1980).

B. Donald and E. Bakies, 'A Glimpse Inside the Brain's Black Box: Understanding the Role of Neuroscience in Criminal Sentencing' (2016) 85 *Fordham Law Review* 481–502.

B. Grey, 'Neuroscience, PTSD, and Sentencing Mitigation' (2012) 34 *Cardozo Law Review* 1–55.

B. Rind and P. Bordia, 'Effect of Server's "Thank You" and Personalization on Restaurant Tipping' (1995) 25 *Journal of Applied Social Psychology* 745–751.

B. Van Der Kolk, *The Body Keeps the Score: Brain, Mind, and Body in the Healing of Trauma* (Penguin Books 2014).

C. Betsey, 'Income and Wealth Transfer Effects of Discrimination in Sentencing' (2005) 32 *The Review of Black Political Economy* 111–120.

C. Delfin et al., 'Prediction of Recidivism in a Long-Term Follow-Up of Forensic Psychiatric Patients' (2019) *PLoS ONE* <https://doi.org/10.1371/journal.pone.0217127>

C. Haney, *Criminality in Context: The Psychological Foundations of Criminal Justice* (APA 2020).

C. Jacobsen and D. Maier-Katkin, 'Breivik's Sanity: Terrorism, Mass Murder, and the Insanity Defense' (2015) 37 *Human Rights Quarterly* 137–152.

C. Keysers, H. Meffert and V. Gazzola, 'Reply: Spontaneous versus Deliberate Vicarious Representations: Different Routes to Empathy in Psychopathy and Autism' (2014) 137 *Brain: A Journal of Neurology* e273.

C. Mackenzie, W. Rogers and S. Dodds, *Vulnerability: New Essays in Ethics and Feminist Philosophy* (Oxford University Press 2013).

C. Wernersen, 'Dette kan bli Breiviks nye hverdag' [This Could Be Breivik's New Everyday Life] (*NRK*, 30 November 2011).

C.-F. Stuckenberg, 'Comparing Legal Approaches: Mental Disorders as Grounds for Excluding Criminal Responsibility' (2016) 4 *Bergen Journal of Criminal Law and Criminal Justice* 48–64.

C. H. de Kogel and E. J. M. C. Westgeest, 'Neuroscientific and Behavioral Genetic Information in Criminal Cases in the Netherlands' (2015) 2(3) *Journal of Law and the Biosciences* 580–605.

C. M. Berryessa and J. Reeves, 'The Perceptions of Juvenile Judges Regarding Adolescent Development in Evaluating Juvenile Competency' (2020) 110 *Journal of Criminal Law and Criminology* 551–592.

C. S. Sergiou et al., 'Transcranial Direct Current Stimulation Targeting the Ventromedial Prefrontal Cortex Reduces Reactive Aggression and Modulates Electrophysiological Responses in a Forensic Population' (2022) 7 *Biol Psychiatry Cogn Neurosci Neuroimaging: CNNI* 95–107.

D. Aono, G. Yaffe and H. Kober, 'Neuroscientific Evidence in the Courtroom: A Review' (2019) 4(40) *Cognitive Res.: Principles and Implication* 1–20.

D. Birks and T. Douglas (eds), *Treatment for Crime* (Oxford University Press 2018).

D. Collins, 'Reevaluating Competence to Stand Trial' (2019) 82 *Law and Contemporary Problems* 157–189.

D. Dante Troutt, 'Trapped in Tragedies: Childhood Trauma,Spatial Inequality, and Law' (2018) 101 *Marquette Law Review* 603–671.

D. Kahneman, O. R. Sibony and C. R. Sunstein, *Noise, A Flaw in Human Judgment* (Little, Brown and Company 2021).

D. Keltner and J. S. Lerner, 'Emotion' in S. T. Fiske and D. T. Gilbert (eds) *Handbook of Social Psychology* Volume 2 (Wiley 2010).

D. Keltner, P. C. Ellsworth and K. Edwards, 'Beyond Simple Pessimism: Effects of Sadness and Anger on Social Perception' (1993) 64 *Journal of Personality and Social Psychology* 740–752.

D. Siegel and M. Solomon (eds), *Healing Trauma: Attachment, Mind, Body, and Brain* (WW Norton & Company 2003).

D. Zimmerman, 'Coercive Wage Offers' (1981) 10 *Philosophy & Public Affairs* 121–145.

D. L. Egbenya and S. Adjorlolo, 'Advancement of Neuroscience and the Assessment of Mental State at the Time of Offense' (2021) 2 *Forensic Science International: Mind and Law* 100046.

D. W. Denno, 'Concocting Criminal Intent' (2017) 105(2) *Georgetown Law Journal* 323–379.

D. W. Denno, 'Empirical Use of Neuroscientific Evidence in Criminal Justice' in S. Della Salla (ed), *The Encyclopedia of Behavioral Neuroscience* (2nd edn, Elsevier 2022).

D. W. Denno, 'How Courts in Criminal Cases Respond to Childhood Trauma' (2019) 103 *Marquette Law Review* 301–363.

D. W. Denno, 'How Experts Have Dominated the Neuroscience Narrative in Criminal Cases for Twelve Decades: A Warning for the Future' (2022) 63 *William & Mary Law Review* 1215–1288.

D. W. Denno, 'Neuroscience and the Personalization of Criminal Law' (2019) 86(2) *The University of Chicago Law Review* 359–401.

D. W. Denno, 'The Myth of the Double-Edged Sword: An Empirical Study of Neuroscience Evidence in Criminal Cases' (2015) 56(2) *Boston College Law Review* 493–551.

D. A. Reify and W. J. Riker (eds), *Coercion and the State* (Springer 2008).

D. J. Harris et al., *Harris, O'Boyle, and Warbrick: Law of the European Convention on Human Rights* (Oxford University Press 2018).

Death Penalty Information Center, 'The Death Penalty in 2022: Year End Report' (16 December, 2022) 22 <https://deathpenaltyinfo.org/facts-and-research/dpic-reports/dpic-year-end-reports/the-death-penalty-in-2022-year-end-report>.

E. Aharoni et al., 'Neuroprediction of Future Rearrest' (2013) 110 *Proceedings of the National Academy of Sciences* 6223–6228.

E. Cauffman and L. Steinberg, 'Emerging Findings from Research on Adolescent Development and Juvenile Justice' (2012) 7 *Victims and Offenders* 428–449.

E. Chaplin et al., 'Severe Mental Illness, Common Mental Disorders, and Neurodevelopmental Conditions Amongst 9088 Lower Court Attendees in London, UK' (2022) 22 *BMC Psychiatry* 551.

E. Dore-Horgan, 'Do Criminal Offenders Have a Right to Neurorehabilitation?' (2022) 17 *Criminal Law and Philosophy* 429–451.

E. Mercurio et al., 'Adolescent Brain Development and Progressive Legal Responsibility in the Latin American Context' (2020) 11 *Frontiers in Psychology* 627.

E. J. Johnson and A. Tversky, 'Affect, Generalization, and the Perception of Risk' (1983) 45 *Journal of Personality and Social Psychology* 20–31.

E. H. Meijer et al., 'Memory Detection with the Concealed Information Test: A Meta-Analysis of Skin Conductance, Respiration Heart Rate and P300 Data' (2014) 51 *Psychophysiology* 879–904.

E. N. Zalta (ed), *The Stanford Encyclopedia of Philosophy* (Summer 2020 Edition)

E. T. E. Higgins and R. M. Sorrentino (eds), *Handbook of Motivation and Cognition*, Volume 2 (1st edn, Guildford Press 1990).

F. Baumgartner et al., 'Racial Resentment and the Death Penalty' (2022) 8 *Journal of Race, Ethnicity, and Politics* 42–60.

F. Coppola, 'The Brain in Solitude: An(other) Eighth Amendment Challenge to Solitary Confinement (2019) 7 *Journal of Law and the Biosciences* 184–225.

F. Coppola, *The Emotional Brain and the Guilty Mind: Novel Paradigms of Culpability and Punishment* (Hart Publishing 2021).

F. Coppola, 'We are More Than our Executive Functions: On the Emotional and Situational Aspects of Criminal Responsibility and Punishment' (2022) 16 *Criminal Law and Philosophy* 253–266.

F. Schauer, *Playing by the Rules: A Philosophical Examination of Rule-Based Decision-Making in Law and in Life* (Clarendon Press 1991).

F. X. Shen, 'Neuroscientific Evidence as Instant Replay' (2016) 3 *Journal of Law and the Biosciences* 343–349.

G. Griffin and S. Sallen, 'Considering Child Trauma Issues in Juvenile Court Sentencing' (2013) 34 *Children's Legal Rights Journal* 1–22.

G. Lamond, 'The Coerciveness of Law' (2000) 20 *Oxford Journal of Legal Studies* 39–62.

G. Loewenstein, 'Out of Control: Visceral Influences on Behavior' (1996) 65 *Organizational Behavior and Human Decision Processes* 272–292.

G. McKeever, 'A Ladder of Legal Participation for Tribunal Users' (2013) 3 *Public Law* 575–598.

G. McKeever et al., 'The Snakes and Ladders of Legal Participation: Litigants in Person and the Right to a Fair Trial Under Article 6 of the European Convention on Human Rights' (2022) 49 *Journal of Law and Society* 71–92.

G. Meynen, 'Brain-Based Mind Reading in Forensic Psychiatry' (2017) 4 *Journal of Law and Biosciences* 311–329.

G. Meynen, *Legal Insanity: Explorations in Psychiatry, Law, and Ethics* (Springer 2016).

G. Meynen, 'Neuroscience-Based Psychiatric Assessments of Criminal Responsibility: Beyond Self-Report?' (2020) 29 *Cambridge Quarterly of Healthcare Ethics* 446–458.

G. Meynen, 'Walls and Laws: Structural Barriers to Forensic Psychiatric Research' (2017) 44 *European Psychiatry* 208–209.

G. Rice and T. Thomas, 'James Bulger - A Matter of Public Interest' (2013) 21 *International Journal of Child Rights* 1–11.

G. Richardson, 'Coercion and Human Rights' (2008) 17 *Journal of Mental Health* 245–254.

G. Szmukler and P. S. Appelbaum, 'Treatment Pressures, Leverage, Coercion, and Compulsion in Mental Health Care' (2008) 17 *Journal of Mental Health* 233–244.

G. Traufetter, 'Experts Disagree on Psychological State of Norwegian Killer' (2011) *Spiegel International*.<https://www.spiegel.de/international/europe/mama-s-boy-and-mass-murderer-experts-disagree-on-psychological-state-of-norwegian-killer-a-805635.html>

G. Tsimploulis et al, 'Schizophrenia and Criminal Responsibility' (2018) 206 *The Journal of Nervous and Mental Disease* 370–377.

G. A. Feigum Pedersen, 'Global funksjonsskåring – Like aktuelt etter siste versjon av diagnosesystemet DSM' [GAF – Just as Relevant After the Latest Version of the Diagnostic System DSM] (2014) 134 *Tidsskrift for Den norske legeforening* 916–917.

G. A. Van Kleef, C. K. De Dreu and A. S. Manstead, 'The Interpersonal Effects of Anger and Happiness in Negotiations' (2004) 86 *Journal of Personality and Social Psychology* 57–76.

G. A. Van Kleef, C. K. De Dreu and A. S. Manstead, 'The Interpersonal Effects of Emotions in Negotiations: A Motivated Information Processing Approach' (2004) 87 *Journal of Personality and Social Psychology* 510–528.

G. McKeever, 'Remote Justice? Litigants in Person and Participation in Court Processes during COVID-19' [2020] *MLRForum* 005 <http://www.modernlawreview.co.uk/mckeever-remote-justice>.

Guide on Article 8 of the European Convention on Human Rights (August 2021).

H. Bless et al., 'Mood and the Use of Scripts: Does a Happy Mood Really Lead to Mindlessness?' (1996) 71 *Journal of Personality and Social Psychology* 665–679..

H. Franke, 'Toxic Stress: Effects, Prevention Treatment' (2014) 1 *Children* 390–402.

H. Howard, 'Effective Participation of Mentally Vulnerable Defendants in the Magistrate Courts in England and Wales – The Front Line from a Legal Perspective' (2021) 85 *The Journal of Criminal Law* 3–16.

H. J. Friendly, 'Some Kind of Hearing' (1975) 123 *University of Pennsylvania Law Review* 1267–1317.

H. Prakken and G. Sartor, 'Law and Logic: A Review from an Argumentation Perspective' (2015) 227 *Artificial Intelligence* 214–245.

H. Teshone, 'The Neural Underlings of Unconscious Racial Biases and Its Effect on Police Behavior' (*CSN*, April 2019) <https://neuroethics.upenn.edu/wp-content/uploads/2019/08/TESHOME_CNS-Final-.pdf>.

HM Courts & Tribunal Services, 'HMCTS Vulnerability Action Plan' Policy Paper (November 2022) <https://www.gov.uk/government/publications/hmcts-vulnerability-action-plan/hmcts-vulnerability-action-plan-october-2022-update>.

I. Andersen, I. Dahl-Nilssen, E.-M. Bulai and A. Moland, 'Krever sakkyndigrevolusjon etter Breivik-saken' [Demands for a Forensic Expertise Revolution After the *Breivik* Case] (*NRK*, 29 February 2012).

I. Melle, 'The Breivik Case and What Psychiatrists Can Learn from It' (2013) 12 *World Psychiatry* 16–21.

J. Briere and C. Scott, 'Complex Trauma in Adolescents and Adults: Effects and Treatment' (2015) 38 *Psychiatric Clinics* 515–527.

J. Clausen and N. Levy (eds), *Handbook of Neuroethics* (Springer Science 2015).

J. Feinberg, *The Moral Limits of the Criminal Law: Volume 3: Harm to Self* (Oxford University Press 1989).

J. Fuss et al., 'Deep Brain Stimulation to Reduce Sexual Drive' (2015) 40 *Journal of Psychiatry Neuroscience* 429–431.

J. Garbarino, 'Foreword: Pathways from Childhood Trauma to Adolescent Violence and Delinquency' (2002) 6 *Journal of Aggression, Maltreatment & Trauma* xxv–xxxi.

J. Garbarino et al., 'Mitigating the Effects of Gun Violence on Children and Youth' (2002) 12 *The Future of Children* 73–85.

J. Griffiths, H. Weyers and M. Adams (eds), *Euthanasia and Law in Europe* (Hart 2008).

J. Gunn, 'No Excuses' (2002) 95 *Journal of the Royal Society of Medicine* 61–63.

J. McEwan, 'Vulnerable Defendants and the Fairness of Trials' (2013) 2 *Criminal Law Review* 100–113.

J. McMillan, 'The Kindest Cut?' (2014) 40 *Journal of Medical Ethics* 583–590.

J. Porcelli and M. R. Delgado, 'Acute Stress Modulates Risk Taking in Financial Decision-Making' (2009) 20 *Psychological Science* 278–283.

J. Rueda and E. Dore-Horgan, 'A Virtual Prosthesis for Morality?' (2022) 13 *AJOB Neuroscience* 163–165.

J. Ryberg, *Neurointerventions, Crime, and Punishment* (Oxford University Press 2020).

J. Sætre and A. Moland, 'Psykiaterne i full splid om Breiviks helsetilstand' [Psychiatrists in Complete Disagreement about Breivik's Health Condition] (*NRK*, 21 December 2011).

J. Zaki, 'Empathy: A Motivated Account' (2014) 140 *Psychological Bulletin* 1608–1647.

J. A. Chandler, 'The Use of Neuroscientific Evidence in Canadian Criminal Proceedings' (2015) 2 *Journal of Law and the Biosciences* 550–579.

J. A. Humbach, 'Do Criminal Minds Cause Crime: Neuroscience and the Physicalism Dilemma' (2019) 12 *Washington University. Jurisprudence Review* 1–26.

J. D. Bremner, 'Traumatic Stress: Effects on the Brain' (2006) 8 *Dialogues in Clinical Neuroscience* 445–461.

J. D. Jackson and S. J. Summers, *The Internationalization of Criminal Evidence* (CUP 2012).

J. D. Wright (eds), *International Encyclopedia of the Social and Behavioral Sciences*, Volume 15 (2nd edn, Elsevier 2015).

J. P. Rosenfeld (ed), *Detecting Concealed Information and Deception: Recent Developments* (Academic Press 2018).

J. R. Simpson (ed), *Neuroimaging in Forensic Psychiatry* (Wiley-Blackwell 2012).

J. S. Lerner et al., 'Emotion and Decision Making' (2015) 66 *Annual Review of Psychology* 799–823.

K. Cunningham, 'Advances in Juvenile Adjudicative Competence: A 10-Year Update' (2020) 38 *Behavioral Sciences & the Law* 406–420.

K. Falch-Nilsen, '«Lex Breivik» kommer 1. juli' [The "Lex Breivik" Is Coming on July 1] (*NRK*, 22 June 2012).

K. Haines et al., 'Children and Crime: In the Moment' (2021) 21 *Youth Justice* 275–298.

K. Olivecrona, *Law as Fact* (Stevens & Sons 1971).

K. Rasmussen, 'Norsk rettsmedisin ved kjøkkenbord og på parkbenker' [Norwegian Forensic Medicine at the Kitchen Table and on Park Benches] (2016) 136 *Tidsskrift for Den Norske Legeforening*.

K. Starcke et al., 'Anticipatory Stress Influences Decision Making under Explicit Risk Conditions' (2008) 122 *Behavioral Neuroscience* 1352–1360.

K. Thomas, 'Beyond Mitigation: Towards a Theory of Allocution' (2007) 75 *Fordham Law Review* 2641–2683.

K. D. Ashley, *Artificial Intelligence and Legal Analytics: New Tools for Law Practice in the Digital Age* (Cambridge University Press 2017).

L. Bortolotti, M. R. Broome and M. Mameli, 'Delusions and Responsibility for Action: Insights from the Breivik Case' (2014) 7 *Neuroethics* 377–382.

L. Gröning et al, 'Constructing Criminal Insanity: The Roles of Legislators, Judges and Experts in Norway, Sweden and the Netherlands' (2020) 11 *New Journal of European Criminal Law* 390–410.

L. Gröning et al, 'Remodelling Criminal Insanity: Exploring Philosophical, Legal, and Medical Premises of the Medical Model used in Norwegian Law' (2022) 81 *International Journal of Law and Psychiatry* 101776.

L. Gröning and G. F. Rieber-Mohn, 'NOU 2014:10 - Proposal for New Rules Regarding Criminal Insanity and Related Issues, Norway Post-22 July' (2015) 3 *Bergen Journal of Criminal Law and Criminal Justice* 109–131.

L. Gröning, U. K. Hansen Haukvik and K. H. Melle 'Criminal insanity, psychosis and impaired reality testing in Norwegian law' (2019) 7 *Bergen Journal of Criminal Law & Criminal Justice* 27–59.

L. Lanfranchi, 'Giusto Processo Nell'enciclopedia Treccani' in *Enciclopedia Giuridica Treccani* (*Institute of the Italian Treccani Encyclopaedia* 2001).

L. Singh, 'Making Progress in the Ethics of Digital and Virtual Technologies for Mental Health' (2022) 13 *AJOB Neuroscience* 141–143.

L. J. Jäggi et al., 'The Relationship between Trauma, Arrest, and Incarceration History among Black Americans: Findings from the National Survey of American Life' (2016) 6 *Society and Mental Health* 187–206.

L. Z. Tiedens and S. Linton, 'Judgment Under Emotional Certainty and Uncertainty: The Effects of Specific Emotions on Information Processing' (2001) 81 *Journal of Personality and Social Psychology* 973–988.

Law Commission, *Unfitness to Plead Volume 1: Report Number 364* (HMSO 2016).

M. Bagaric, 'Rich Offender, Poor Offender: Why It (Sometimes) Matter in Sentencing' (2015) 33 *Minnesota Journal of Law & Inequality* 1–51.

M. Bagaric et al., 'Trauma and Sentencing: The Case for Mitigating Penalty for Childhood Physical and Sexual Abuse' (2019) 30 *Stanford Law & Policy Review* 1–59.

M. Bove, 'Art. 111 Cost. e "Giusto Processo Civile"' *Rivista di diritto processuale*, Volume 57 (Associazione ESSPER periodici italiani di economia, scienze sociali e storia 2002).

M. Fjellvang, L. Gröning and U. K. Haukvik, 'Imaging Violence in Schizophrenia: A Systematic Review and Critical Discussion of the MRI Literature' (2018) 9 *Frontiers in Psychiatry* 333.

M. Gohara, 'In Defense of the Injured: How Trauma-Informed Criminal Defense Can Reform Sentencing' (2018) 45 *American Journal of Criminal Law* 1–53.

M. Gohara, 'Grace Notes: A Case for Making Mitigation the Heart of Noncapital Sentencing' 41 *American Journal of Criminal Law* 41–89.

M. Hafner, 'Judging Homicide Defendants by Their Brains: An Empirical Study on the Use of Neuroscience in Homicide Trials in Slovenia' (2019) 6 *Journal of Law and the Biosciences* 226–254.

M. Manikis, 'Recognising State Blame in Sentencing: A Communicative and Relational Framework' (2022) 81 *The Cambridge Law Journal* 294–322.

M. Mindestrømmen, 'Impending Danger: The Meaning of Danger as a Legal Requirement for Involuntary Psychiatric Treatment in the Norwegian Criminal Justice System' (2019) 7 *Bergen Journal of Criminal Law & Criminal Justice* 110–135.

M. Vikås, E. B. Utheim and M. S. Hopperstad, 'Rieber-Mohn: – Aldri opplevd dette før' [Rieber-Mohn: I Never Experienced this Before] (*VG*, 24 May 2012).

M. D. White (ed), *The Insanity Defense: Multidisciplinary Views on its History, Trends and Controversies* (Praeger 2017).

M. S. Moore, 'The Quest for a Responsible Responsibility Test: Norwegian Insanity Law after Breivik' (2015) 9 *Criminal Law and Philosophy* 645–693.

M. T. Berg and R. Loeber, 'Examining the Neighborhood Context of the Violent Offending-Victimization Relationship: A Prospective Investigation' (2011) 27 *Journal of Quantitative Criminology* 427–451.

M. J. Blitz, 'Extended Reality, Mental Liberty, and State Power in Forensic Settings' (2022) 13 *AJOB Neuroscience* 173–176.

N. Adams et al., 'The Relationship Between Childhood Traumatic Experiences and Gang-Involved Delinquent Behavior in Adolescent Boys' (2009) 6 *Journal of the American Academy of Special Education Professionals* 6–16.

N. Lacey, 'Socializing the Subject of Criminal Law? Criminal Responsibility and the Purposes of Criminalization' (2016) 99 *Marquette Law Review* 541–557.

N. A. Vincent, T. Nadelhoffer and A. McCay (eds), *Neurointerventions and the Law: Regulating Human Mental Capacity* (Oxford University Press 2020).

National Child Traumatic Stress Network, 'Trauma in the Lives of Gang-Involved Youth: Tips for Volunteers and Community Organizations' (2009).

Norwegian Parliament, 'Session of Monday 11 June 2012 at 10.00. Issue nr. 1. Transcript' <https://www.stortinget.no/no/Saker-og-publikasjoner/Publikasjoner/Referater/Stortinget/2011–2012/120611/1>.

NOU 2014: 10, *Criminal Capacity, (Forensic-Psychiatric) Expertise and Societal Protection* <https://www.regjeringen.no/no/dokumenter/NOU-2014-10/id2008986/>.

O. Choy, F. Focquaert and A. Raine, 'Benign Biological Interventions to Reduce Offending' (2020) 13 *Neuroethics* 29–41.

O. Rollins, *Conviction: The Making and Unmaking of the Violent Brain* (Stanford University Press 2021).

O. D. Jones, et al., 'Law and Neuroscience' (2013) 33 *The Journal of Neuroscience* 17624–17630.

O. D. Jones, J. D. Schall and F. X. Shen, *Law and Neuroscience* (2nd edn, Aspen Publishing 2020).

P. Brown et al., 'Prevalence of Mental Disorders in Defendants at Criminal Court' (2022) 8 *BJPsych Open* 1–8.

P. Catley and L. Claydon, 'The Use of Neuroscientific Evidence in the Courtroom by Those Accused of Criminal Offenses in England and Wales' (2015) 2 *Journal of Law and the Biosciences* 510–549.

P. Cooper and J. Grace, 'Vulnerable Patients Going to Court: A Psychiatrist's Guide to Special Measures' (2016) 40 *BJPsych Bulletin* 220–222.

P. Daniluk (ed), *Patient Autonomy and Criminal Law: European Perspectives* (Routledge 2023).

P. Jacobs, *Force-Feeding of Prisoners and Detainees on Hunger Strike* (Intersentia 2012).

P. Kellmeyer, N. Biller-Andorno and G. Meynen, 'Ethical Tensions of Virtual Reality Treatment in Vulnerable Patients' (2019) 25 *Nature Medicine* 1185–1188.

P. van Dijk et al. (eds), *Theory and Practice of the European Convention on Human Rights* (Intersentia 2018).

P.-A. Johansen and A. Bakke-Foss, 'Eksperter tviler på grunnlaget for Behring Breiviks diagnose' [Experts Question the Basis for Behring Breivik's Diagnosis] (*Aftenposten*, 4 December 2011).

P. J. Løvgren and P. T. Wiig, 'Farlige, syke personer – Hjelpetrengende eller "tikkende bomber"?' [Dangerous, Sick Persons: Vulnerable People or "Ticking Bombs"?] (2022) 13 *Tidsskriftet for Den norske legeforeniging*.

P. J. Løvgren et al, 'Use of Assessment Instruments in Forensic Evaluations of Criminal Responsibility in Norway' (2022) 22 *BMC Psychiatry* 1–14.

P. L. Crocker, 'Childhood Abuse and Adult Murder: Implications for the Death Penalty' (1999) 77 *North Carolina Law Review* 1143–1222.

P. S. Appelbaum, 'A Theory of Ethics for Forensic Psychiatry' (1997) 25 *Journal of the American Academy of Psychiatry and the Law Online* 233–247.

P. R. Roelfsema, D. Denys and P. C. Klink, 'Mind Reading and Writing: The Future of Neurotechnology' (2018) 22 *Trends in Cognitive Sciences* 598–610.

R. Adolphs and D. J. Anderson, *The Neuroscience of Emotion: A New Synthesis* (Princeton University Press 2018).

R. Arthur, 'Giving Effect to Young People's Right to Participate Effectively in Criminal Proceedings' (2016) 28 *Child and Family Law Quarterly* 223–238.

R. Arthur and T. Crofts, 'The Use of Intermediaries for Young Defendants: Overcoming Barriers to Young People's Participation in Criminal Proceedings' (2022) 34 *Child and Family Law Quarterly* 149–168.

R. Cipes, S. Bernstein and E. Hall (eds), *Criminal Defense Techniques* § 32.01(1)(e) (Matthew Bender & Co 2018).

R. Duff, 'Law, Language and Community: Some Preconditions of Criminal Liability' (1998) 2 *Oxford Journal of Legal Studies* 189–206.

R. Faden, T. L. Beauchamp and N. M. P. King, *A History and Theory of Informed Consent* (Oxford University Press 1986).

R. Mackay and W. Brookbanks (eds), *The Insanity Defence: International and Comparative Perspectives* (Oxford University Press 2022).

R. C. Hughes, 'Law and Coercion' (2013) 8 *Philosophy Compass* 231–240.

R. K. Helm, 'Guilty Pleas in Children: Legitimacy, Vulnerability, and the Need for Increased Protection' (2021) 48 *Journal of Law and Society* 179–201.

S. Aiyer et al., 'Exposure to Violence Predicting Cortisol Response During Adolescence and Early Adulthood: Understanding Moderating Factors' (2014) 43 *Journal of Youth and Adolescence* 1066–1079.

S. Anderson, 'Coercion' in E. N. Zalte (ed), *The Stanford Encyclopedia of Philosophy* (Summer 2021 Edition).

S. Bloch and S. A. Green (eds), *Psychiatric Ethics* (4th ed, Oxford University Press 2009).

S. Buckingham, 'Trauma-Informed Juvenile Justice' (2016) 53 *American Journal of Criminal Law Review* 641–692.

S. Han, J. S. Lerner and D. Keltner, 'Feelings and Consumer Decision Making: The Appraisal-Tendency Framework' (2007) 17 *Journal of Consumer Psychology* 158–168.

S. LaVelle Ficke, K. J. Hart and P. A. Deardorff, 'The Performance of Incarcerated Juveniles on the MacArthur Competence Assessment Tool-Criminal Adjudication (MacCAT-CA)' (2006) 34 *The Journal of the American Academy of Psychiatry and the Law* 360–373.

S. Ligthart, *Coercive Brain-Reading in Criminal Law* (Cambridge University Press 2022).

S. Ligthart et al., 'Closed-Loop Brain Devices in Offender Rehabilitation' (2021) 30 *Cambridge Quarterly Healthcare Ethics* 669–680.

S. Lupien et al., 'Effects of Stress Throughout the Lifespan on the Brain, Behavior and Cognition' (2009) 10 *Nature Reviews* 434–445.

S. Lightart et al., 'Prison and the Brain: Neuropsychological Research in the Light of the European Convention of Human Rights' (2019) 10 *New Journal of European Criminal Law* 287–300.

S. Moratti and D. Patterson (eds), *Legal Insanity and the Brain: Science, Law and European Courts* (Bloomsbury 2016).

S. Morgenbesser, P. Suppes and M. White (eds), *Philosophy, Science, and Method Essays in Honor of Ernest Nagel* (St. Martin's Press 1969).

S. Wessely, 'Anders Breivik, the Public, and Psychiatry' (2012) 379 *The Lancet* 1563–1564.

S. A. Skålevåg, 'The Irresponsible Criminal in Norwegian Medico-Legal Discourse' (2014) 37 *International Journal of Law and Psychiatry* 82–90.

S. F. Cole et al., 'Mass Advocates for Children, Helping Traumatized Children Learn: Supportive School Environments for Children Traumatized by Family Violence' (2005) <https://traumasensitiveschools.org/wp-content/uploads/2013/06/Helping-Traumatized-Children-Learn.pdf>.

SIFER, *Sikkerhetpsykiatri i Norge 2019* [Security Psychiatry in Norway 2019] (SIFER South-East 2020).

Substance Abuse and Mental Health Service Administration (SAMHSA), *Trauma and Violence* <https://www.samhsa.gov/trauma-violence>.

T. Brosch, 'The Impact of Emotion on Perception, Attention, Memory, and Decision-Making' [2013] *Swiss Medical Weekly.*

T. Douglas et al., 'Coercion, Incarceration, and Chemical Castration' (2013) 10 *Journal of Bioethical Inquiry* 393–405.

T. Grisso, et al., '"Juveniles" Competence to Stand Trial: A Comparison of Adolescents' and Adults' Capacities as Trial Defendants' (2003) 27 *Law & Human Behavior* 333–363.

T. Grisso and R. G. Schwartz (eds), *Youth on Trial: A Developmental Perspective on Juvenile Justice* (University of Chicago Press 2000).

T. Spranger (ed), *International Neurolaw: A Comparative Analysis* (Springer-Verlag 2012).

T. R. Birkhead and K. R. Guest Pryal, 'Symposium 2014: Vulnerable Defendants in the Criminal Justice System' (2015) 93 *North Carolina Law Review* 1211–1223.

The Empathic Brain (YouTube 2018) can be found here <https://www.youtube.com/watch?v=Yw8p2D2Jejg>.

The Sentencing Project, 'Racial Disparity in Sentencing' (January 2005) <https://www.opensocietyfoundations.org/publications/racial-disparity-sentencing>.

V. Buan, P.-A. Holm, A. Bakke Foss and A. Færaas, 'Sakkyndige konkluderer med at Behring Breivik er tilregnelig' [The Experts Conclude that Behring Breivik Is Criminally Accountable] (*Aftenposten,* 10 April 2012).

W. Buelens, C. Herijgers and S. Illegems, 'The View of the European Court of Human Rights on Competent Patients' Right of Informed Consent' (2016) 23 *European Journal of Health Law* 481–509.

W. G. Jennings et al., 'On the Overlap Between Victimization and Offending: A Review of the Literature' (2012) 17 *Aggression and Violent Behavior* 16–26.1

W. O. Holmes Jr, 'The Common Law 1881' Lecture I.

Z. N. Edward, *Stanford Encyclopedia of Philosophy* (Fall 2020 Edition).

Index

For Product Safety Concerns and Information please contact our EU
representative GPSR@taylorandfrancis.com
Taylor & Francis Verlag GmbH, Kaufingerstraße 24, 80331 München, Germany

www.ingramcontent.com/pod-product-compliance
Lightning Source LLC
Chambersburg PA
CBHW061333220326
41599CB00026B/5160

9 781032 362700